god has no religion

god has no religion

blending traditions for prayer

frances sheridan goulart

 SORIN BOOKS Notre Dame, Indiana

Acknowledgments are listed on pp. 250–252.

www.sorinbooks.com

International Standard Book Number: 1-893732-74-6

Cover and text design by Katherine Robinson Coleman

Photography: Photodisc 45, 66, 82, 143, 163, 183, 203, 228, 243.

Liquid Library 138.

Colin Moore, www.hitherandyononline.com: 223.

Jeff Saward, www.labyrintho.net: 126.

Nancy Jane Reid, www.newportnet.com/archives/mandala/nancy/home.htm: 71.

Printed and bound in the United States of America.

Library of Congress Cataloging-in-Publication Data

Goulart, Frances Sheridan.
  God has no religion : blending traditions for prayer / Frances Sheridan Goulart.
    p. cm.
  Includes bibliographical references.
  ISBN 1-893732-74-6 (pbk.)
  1. Prayer. 2. Prayers. I. Title.

BL560.G68 2005
204'.33—dc22
                                         2004024012

To that cloud of witnesses in my life who have been so uncommonly supportive. Among them are my friends at Pax Christi Metro New York, the sisters at the Community of the Holy Spirit, and fellow teachers of the dispersed Yoga sangha in Connecticut.

To Ronnie,

William,

and

Chas

for their lessons

in faith

and

courage

over the years.

contents

Prayers
and
Praying
in the
Twenty-First Century:

what,

where,

how,

and

to whom

we pray

In the words of Mohandas Gandhi, "God has no religion."

He (She, The One, They) is alive and well in our worship. We're saying our prayers, but not always in the same ways, in the same places, or with the same-old same-old intent. We have become increasingly syncretistic, not abandoning our beliefs, but blending various beliefs and practices. According to Rabbi Howard A. Addison, author of *Show Me Your Way*, a survey that tracked a large number of adults who were confirmed in a variety of churches during the 1960s revealed that twenty years later only one-third had remained within their denomination. Eight out of ten respondents thought one's religious beliefs should be arrived at independent of any religious institution, while seven out of ten felt that all religions were equally valid ways to find ultimate truth.

In other words, twenty-first century seekers revere the past but aren't held hostage by it. Almost half of all Americans under thirty, and one-third of those over seventy, think the best religion is one that borrows from all religions. We are on many paths these days other than the ones inscribed and sanctified by institutionalized religion.

And we are no longer one *Christian* nation under God. Nationwide there are more Buddhists than Presbyterians or Episcopalians, and there are nearly as many Muslim Americans as Jewish Americans. Additionally, the United States is home to about one million Hindus and 300,000 Sikhs, according to the Pluralism Project at Harvard University. Indeed in 1998, New York's Open Center drew a quarter of a million seekers to a wide range of workshops in everything from kabbalah and mysticism, to Buddhism, Baha'i, and tantric sexuality. Is it any wonder, asks the rabbi (whose spiritual director is a Roman Catholic nun), that many Americans blend their own mix of traditions, calling themselves "Episcopalian-practicing non-Jew" or "Mennonite-Unitarian-Universalist Zen Meditator" or the increasingly popular JewBu (Jewish Buddhist)?

We are praying in numbers, but not *by* the numbers. Despite the suspicion that society is headed for hell in a handbasket, 21 percent of us think we are *more* spiritual than our elders, and 49 percent think we are equally as moved by the spirit as those elders. This survey gives support to the observation that we don't pray because God needs it, but because *we* do.

We are moved to pray in different places and spaces and even in different positions. We may not save our prayers for the church, temple, or synagogue anymore. We may, in fact, be doing our "God talk" in the garden, at the beach, on a bike, or during a hike. Or we may be *crossover worshipers*, praying in the standard locations *and* on the commuter train.

We aren't just *saying* our prayers these days. We're sweating them, singing them, walking them, humming them, chanting them, signing them, breathing them, and even growing them. And it isn't just standard issue prayers that are fueling our spiritual lives. It is meditations, mantras, embodied prayer, labyrinth walking, affirmations, blessings, and engaged silence. God exists, as Buddhists tell us, when man lets Him or Her in; and prayer of any kind offers that opening.

This book is for *anyone* looking to get out of his or her devotional comfort zone, with creeds that are more nuanced, canons that are cross-traditionally blended, and prayer rituals that take us outside our sacred box. These prayers have been collected from a wide spectrum of spiritual sources, with plenty of variations, options, and rituals to learn about and try for yourself. *God Has No Religion* also offers the option of inclusive language throughout and, even better, a wide range of names for God (all images of God being, after all, limited and partial), contributing a much needed richness to our liturgies still top-heavy with *heavenly fathers*.

"Take from us all lukewarmness in meditation, dullness in prayer," Saint Thomas More begged. I hope that this book will help to save you from all "dullness in prayer." For, as author-seeker Karen Armstrong has observed, "By learning to pray the prayers of people who do not share our beliefs we can learn at a level deeper than creedal, to value their faith."

Let us pray.

Don't worry about anything,
but pray about everything.
Philippians 4:6

Down on Our Knees, Up on Our Toes:

prayer practices

and the

prayerware

to go

with them

Just as there are countless prayers, there are countless common, and not so common, ways to pray. These ways include the physical positions in which we say or practice our devotions as well as the tools, or prayerware, we use once we assume that position. While nothing more than our presence and a prayerful intent is essential to devotion, whatever improves our ability to focus or open our heart can't be bad. Here are a few of those tools and practices drawn from a variety of spiritual traditions.

Practices

Lectio Divina

Lectio divina, or sacred reading, is a method of praying scripture which was originally conceived as a Christian practice but which can be applied to any prayer practice. Simply begin by centering yourself in God's abiding presence. Lighting a candle or incense, listening to a piece of meditative music, or simply sitting in silence for a few moments can help set the mood. Next select the scripture or prayer of your choice and begin to read it slowly, absorbing each word, hearing beyond the page. When you come to a word or passage that speaks to you, stop, read it again, and get comfortable with it. Read it aloud to bring it to life. Reflect on the meaning and pray for guidance in applying the message to your life. Additionally, you may choose to record your thoughts in a prayer journal. It is customary to close a session of *lectio* after ten, fifteen, or twenty minutes with your favorite mantra, a deep bow, or simply by blessing yourself. The ritual is yours. Be creative in any way that deepens the practice for you.

Mantra

"My greatest weapon," said Mohandas Gandhi, "is mute prayer." Indeed, Hindus believe that when that special prayer, called a mantra (literally, "something to lean the mind on"), is repeated a hundred or even a thousand times a day and the believer makes the effort to identify with the worshiped, the power of that deity will come to his or her help. There is a world in a word, or a string of sacred words. What that special word is differs for each tradition and believer. In many Asian countries, mantras are still chanted in the original Sanskrit (considered the language of the Gods). Mantras—anything from *Om* to *Maranatha* (Sanskrit for "The Lord cometh")—help to focus, stabilize, and free the mind and heart. Mantras can also be combined with mindful breathing, visualizations, and the use of prayer beads to keep track of the number of repetitions. Christians may use the Hail Mary prayer ("Hail Mary full of grace, the Lord is with you. Blessed are you among women and blessed is the fruit of your womb, Jesus"), the Christian Breath mantra ("Breathe through me, Breath of God, fill me with life anew"), or the Jesus prayer ("Lord Jesus, Son of the living God, have mercy on me, a sinner") which comes from the Greek and Orthodox tradition where it is known as the Prayer of the Heart. Muslims may repeat the numerous names of *Allah*, while Buddhists may use the prayer of the Lord Buddha, *Om Mani Padme Hum*.

To use a mantra, pause to center yourself, find stillness within, and repeat your chosen word(s) at fixed or random intervals throughout the day. It is said that the one who prays is eventually transformed into the prayer itself and begins to reflect to others the compassion, love, and nonviolence of Jesus, Buddha, or the spirit who is invoked.

Consider using a mantra to celebrate your own version of the Muslim call to prayer, *Salaat*, a ritual of prayer five times daily in which mind, body, and heart turn toward God. Or, in the Orthodox Judaic manner, divide the day into three major periods, pausing for five or ten minutes during each period to mindfully repeat your chosen mantra.

Arrow Prayer

Arrow prayers are brief meditations (usually one or two lines) of praise, petition, or affirmation. Some examples are: "Create a clean heart in me, O Lord" (Psalm 51) and "*Barukh atah Adonai, Elohaynu, melekh ha-olam*" ("Blessed are you Lord, Our God, King of the Universe" in Hebrew). Arrow prayers can be used when you need instant action, such as a quick prayer for help in a difficult situation.

Labyrinth

A labyrinth may be the next best thing to a pilgrimage. A tool for meditation in motion, it is common to many religious traditions and has become a symbol (like the mandala) of the spiritual journey. Forming one intriguing winding path that proceeds from the edge of a circle (usually forty feet in diameter in full-scale models) to the center and then back out again, walking this ancient path calms the mind, balances the body, and refreshes the soul.

.The origin of the labyrinth isn't certain. The oldest existing example, believed to date from 2500–2000 B.C., is at Knossos on the island of Crete. The world's best-known labyrinth, dating back to 1220, is located on the floor of Chartres Cathedral near Paris, France.

As you walk from the outer to the inner core (representing your Higher Power) and back again, you make a conscious effort to release what is no longer useful to you in your life. After pausing at the apex, to receive whatever the Holy One may be offering you, you prayerfully retrace your steps to the starting point, using this journey to integrate any new insights.

The journey is yours to shape and experience in any way that nourishes your soul. You might carry prayer beads or a wrist mala to help you repeat your mantra. Or walk to deepen your own loving kindness, sending it out to all sentient beings with each step. Or make the trip a mindful meditation, focusing completely on each step and on every sensation it brings. If you live in the vicinity of a house of worship that has a full-sized labyrinth, make a regular walk a part of your prayer life.

In addition to the brick and concrete institutional models, there are smaller portable "finger" labyrinths made of canvas or wood for indoor use (perfect for traveling). Consider sharing the purchase with a prayer partner.

Prayer Walking or Walking Meditation

In this practice, you become the prayer, concentrating your full attention on the movement and placement of the leg and the foot as you walk outdoors or trace a chosen path inside (consider your house of worship, community center, a mall during quiet times, etc.). Emptying the mind of all mental activity, surrender totally to the present moment. Breathe consciously, matching your breath to each slow step, listening for the voice of God.

Prayer walking can put you in touch with the people and purposes that propel you forward in life. As you walk, you become more conscious of the landscape you may know but may not have acknowledged or received on a deeper level. You are slowing your prayer life down to a walk, getting in touch with the mystery of what's around you, under your feet, before your eyes. Regular practitioners (who also call this a "slow walk") suggest walking at a moderate pace, then slowing down and walking even more slowly. Your mind will gradually become more alert and your decisions will be made with more insight and compassion.

Inner Light Meditation

Inner light meditation or simple candle flame meditation (known to yogis as *Tratak*) is a practice from Tibetan Buddhism which encourages the meditator through steady gazing to feel more open and spacious. The object is usually the flickering flame of a candle, but a painting of a deity, an icon, or a mandala may be used. You may also use what is known in yogic meditation as a *yantra*, a geometric diagram that focuses the mind and is imbued with a mystic meaning.

Light a candle in a darkened room, setting it at eye level, about two feet from where you will be sitting. Get comfortable and begin breathing in and out quietly and rhythmically. Let the body relax, softening the breath. Concentrate only on the flickering light (or other object). Watch it steadily for several minutes without thinking of anything. Try to let your mind move into the flame or object. As you meditate on the candle flame or other chosen object, imagine it expanding beyond the body and shining forth into eternity, suffusing and transforming the world around you. Then blow out the candle, close your eyes. See the after-image that forms on the inside of your eyelids. Meditate on that image. With practice, it is said that the mind ceases to exist as an individual entity and merges back into its source.

Prayer Journaling

Journaling can be an adjunct to prayer or a meditative practice itself. Use your journal to reflect on the words you have just prayed or on your spiritual progress this day. Better yet, write a letter to God, a practice that gives you a "from-my-pen-to-your-ear, God" feeling and a record of your daily practice. What comes from the hand, as they say, often comes from the heart.

Prayerware

Prayer Beads

Praying can sometimes get better with props. Prayer beads such as the Catholic rosary, the Eastern Orthodox prayer rope, and the Buddhist mala are common to several traditions including Islam, Hinduism, Native American, and African Masai. And they can be adapted to any prayer practice.

Simply fingering the beads can be a prompt to fall into reverent silence; the use of beads symbolizes the commitment to the spiritual life.

The first beads, dating back forty thousand years, used grooved pebbles, bones, and teeth. The ancient Egyptians' use of beads (called *sha sha* or luck) dates back to 3200 B.C. The third century Desert Mothers and Fathers carried pebbles which they dropped one by one on the ground as they recited their prayers. Traditionally, beads have consisted of strings of like-sized beads, seeds, and even beads made of crushed rose petals (from which comes the term *rosary*). While the rosary consists of five decades (the 150 beads were used originally to count the reciting of the 150 psalms in the Bible), the *mala* (Sanskrit for "rose" or "garland") used by Hindus is available in long and short versions. The long mala has 108 beads (a sacred number, said to represent the number of earthly desires which afflict mortals), with one bead as the summit bead called a *sumeru* or *guru*. Wrist malas have twenty-two or twenty-seven beads or nine large ones.

You can make your own mala or rosary to reflect your own personal approach to string-a-prayer spirituality. Consider using a cross you've had since childhood, beads from a rosary or mala you received on some special occasion, and other symbols of times you wish to commemorate. Using bead stringing materials like elastic or wire, you can add pebbles or stones to your string. You can create different sets of beads to reflect different spiritual goals, people, or events in your life; or make an open-ended rosary, adding a bead each time you overcome an obstacle. Last, create a ceremony to bless your beads, or have them blessed by a spiritual advisor, priest, rabbi, etc. Another homemade way to sanctify your beads is to dip them in a stream, a river, or the ocean.

Mandala

Mandala is the Sanskrit word for "circle." It is a symbol for wholeness and is seen as a cosmic diagram reminding us of our relation to the world that extends both beyond and within our minds and bodies. Mandala-making is a form of meditation.

In eastern religions such as Buddhism, Jainism, and Hinduism, the mandala is a tool for transformation. Tibetan monks create intricate mandalas with colored sand which are later destroyed to demonstrate the impermanence of all things. Similarly, American Navajo create temporary sand paintings which are used in religious rituals.

When you create your mandala you are echoing the universal circle seen throughout nature, and no two are ever alike. Start with a sheet of paper, and use crayons, paints, or colored pencils to create representations of your spirit, your world, and your faith. Decide what or who is at the middle of your mandala. Find a way to represent what you need at this time to keep you on the path. Mandalas can also be created using colored sand, beads, stones, and other art materials.

Singing Bowls

Tibetan Buddhists use exotic singing bowls, so called because of the richly resonant humming vibrations they give off when a wooden mallet is traced around the inside rim, to call meditators to prayer. Traditionally forged from an alloy of seven metals, every bowl was handcrafted with a distinct character and quality of its own. It is thought that singing bowls may have played a role in shamanic ritual before the introduction of Buddhism to Tibet. Today, they can be used as musical instruments or as aids to meditation and prayer. It is also thought that the vibrational qualities of the bowl can help restore harmony in our bodies.

Cymbals, Chimes, and Bells

Cymbals, chimes, and bells are used to mark the beginning and end of meditation or prayer as well as to clear the space of negative energy and help quiet the mind.

Saucer shaped cymbals, called *tingshas,* have long been used during the chanting of mantras, prayers, and songs by Buddhist monks, nuns, and yogis. When the two metal disks are struck together, they produce a unique shimmering sound. Consider small tabletop chimes (often crafted from individually tuned temple bells) which are rung by falling beads, or look for temple (hand) bells, of various sizes, used in both eastern and western traditions, to keep on your altar or at your prayer mat/place.

Other items of prayerware that may be useful to your devotional practice include candles, incense, meditation cushions, a prayer rug, and a prayer shawl. Also consider choosing a secluded spot in your home to set up as your prayer corner or altar. Keep your prayerware in that location, so that each time you pass it you will be reminded to pray.

The Amen Corner:

greetings

and

goodbyes

What is the best, most graceful, most reverent, and/or most fitting way to close a prayer?

Amen (Hebrew for "So be it") may be the most familiar to most pray-ers, but it isn't the only devotional exit strategy. A new ending may be a good beginning to praying in a new or renewed way. Whatever your spiritual path, there's nothing to stop you from saying a prayer in one tradition and closing it in another. What matters is that God is always listening, no matter what the language, hour, or approach.

Alleluia: from the Hebrew for "Praise Ye Jehovah."

Baptizus Sum: Latin for "I am baptized." This is how Martin Luther began his prayer time each day, but it also serves as an excellent way to close a prayer, immersed in your faith.

Blessed Be: A Feminist way of blessing what has passed and what's to come.

By All That Is Sacred and True, So Mote [Might] It Be: Used in Wiccan and Earth religions to close prayers. You may use only the first or the last half as an Amen.

Ho: A Native American salutation and Amen alternative.

I Ask This for Myself, My People, and All My Relations: Native Americans use this lengthy Amen alternative to reflect their belief in the interrelatedness of all creation, from the Family of Man/Woman to the mineral kingdom.

Jai Bhagwan: Sanskrit for "I bow to the light within you."

Kyrie Eleison: "Lord have mercy" in Latin.

May Peace Prevail on Earth: The World Peace Prayer Society's all-purpose arrow prayer.

Namaste: Sanskrit for "The light within me honors the light within you."

Om: Considered the most sacred syllable in the literature of Hinduism, Om is thought to be the eternal sound of the universe; it is said to stand for Brahman, the eternal spirit whom Hindus call God.

Om Mani Padme Hum: The essence of Buddhist teachings, the Om consists of what are called "the six perfections." Through practice one can achieve perfection in:

Om	generosity
Ma	pure ethics
Ni	tolerance and patience
Pad	perseverance
Me	concentration
Hum	wisdom

Peace

Praise Be

Ram, Ram, Ram: A Hindu invocation of God. Use to open or close any prayer.

Salaam: "Peace" in Arabic. The word is usually said with a deep bow, right palm touching the forehead.

Shalom: "Peace" in Hebrew.

Shanti: "Peace" (or inner peace through understanding) in Sanskrit. Shanti is often used with Om and customarily repeated three times, as in, Om Shanti, Shanti, Shanti.

Spiritus Sanctus: Latin, another way of saying Blessed Be.

Svaha: "Amen" in Sanskrit. In Native American, it is translated as "Waiting for promises to be fulfilled."

You may choose any alternative to Amen that you like. And you can use a different one each time you pray. You have the final word, so make it a good one.

Prayers

Prayers
of the Day

An Alternative Lord's Prayer

O Birther! Father-Mother of the Cosmos,

Focus your light within us—make it useful:

Create your reign of unity now—

Your one desire then acts with ours,

As in all light, so in all forms.

Grant what we need each day in bread and insight.

Loose the cords of mistakes binding us,

As we release the strands we hold

Of others' guilt.

Don't let surface things delude us,

But free us from what holds us back.

From you is born all ruling will,

The power and the life to do,

The song that beautifies all,

From age to age it renews.

Truly—power to these statements—

May they be the ground from which all

My actions grow.

Amen.

Origin:

Translated from the original Aramaic version of the Our Father by Neil Douglas-Klotz, co-chair of the Mysticism Group of the American Academy of Religion and founder of the International Network for the Universal Dances of Peace.

Options:

- If you say the more traditional Our Father (also known as the Lord's Prayer), alternate it with this version occasionally.

- Choose one line as a mantra/focus throughout the day or for a meditation practice.

Tradition/Path: Christian Science

Thy Kingdom Come

Thy kingdom come,

Let the reign of divine truth, life and love be established in me,

And rule out of me all sin;

And may Thy Word enrich the affections of all mankind,

And govern them.

Origin:

Mary Baker Eddy (1821–1910), the founder of the Church of Christ, Scientist (Christian Science) and author of the spiritual classic *Science and Health*. She believed that there was a "science" behind Jesus' healing method, and that it was "divinely natural and repeatable."

Options:

- Use this as an alternative to the Our Father.

- Experiment with different positions for prayer. If you always pray kneeling, try standing. If you usually pray while seated in a chair, move to a meditation cushion on the floor. Try the Islamic tradition of praying while alternating between kneeling and prostration.

Tradition/Path: Celtic Christian

O God of Life

O God of life, this night

O darken not to me thy light,

O God of life, this night

Close not thy gladness to my sight.

O God of life, this night

Thy door to me, O shut not tight,

O God of life, this night.

Origin:

An excerpt from the Northumbria Community's Cuthbert Compline (seventh century). The Northumbria Community is an Irish order that mixes Celtic Christianity and monasticism in their continuing quest for a "new monasticism."

Options:

- Celtic Christians were largely illiterate and would not have read this prayer, but would certainly have recited it aloud. Try singing this naturally lilting prayer.

- This may be recited using prayer beads, repeating the prayer as many times as you have beads. If you wear a wrist mala, you can pray without ceasing throughout the day, keeping track by fingering the beads on your wrist.

Tradition/Path: Catholic Christian

Light

O God,

Who divides the day from the night,

Separate our deeds from the gloom of darkness,

That ever meditating on things holy,

We may continually live in your light.

Origin:

Leonine Sacramentary, fifth century. Sacramentaries were the earliest sources for the Roman Rite (canon of the Mass). The Leonine, named for Pope Leo I, is one of the three earliest, complete, and important of the sacramentaries.

Options:

- Use this as an evening prayer.

- As an encouragement to meditate on holy things, carry a prayer stone in your pocket. Stop to pray this prayer (or another meditation) whenever you reach into your pocket to find this devotional reminder. If you have several smooth stones, you can use acrylic paint or a permanent marker to inscribe each with a "spirit word" (love, adoration, humility, etc.) as a reminder of a virtue you are working on.

Reveal Yourself

Almighty *and ever living God,*

You are beyond the grasp of our highest thought,

But within the reach of our frailest trust;

Come in the beauty of the morning's light and

Reveal Yourself to us.

Enrich us out of the heritage of seers and scholars
and saints

Into whose faith and labors we have entered.

And quicken us to new insights for our time;

That we may be possessors of the truth of many

Yesterdays, partakers of your thoughts for today,

And creators with you of a better tomorrow;

Through Jesus Christ, the Lord of the ages.

Origin:

Henry Sloane Coffin (1877–1954), Presbyterian
minister, author, and educator. He led the movement
for liberal evangelicalism in the Protestant churches.

Options:

- If you are not Christian, omit the italicized lines,
  adding your own salutation.

- If praying solo, change "we," "us," and "our" to "I," "me," and "my."

- Use this as a morning prayer.

- If you keep a prayer journal, reflect on the meaning for you of "creators with you of a better tomorrow." How can your life reflect this intention?

Lord, one day I will live with you where you are. May you live with me where I am now.

John Mason Neale

Hail Mother

Hail Mother, who are the earth,

Hallowed by thy soil, rocks and flora,

That nourish and support all life.

Blessed be thy wind that gives us breath

And thy waters that quench, bathe, and refresh

All living things.

Holy Earth—as one—we praise your majesty,

Grace, and wonder.

Origin:

Bill Faherty

Options:

- Pause as you recite the italicized line. Close your eyes and breathe slowly and rhythmically, in and out. Feel God breathe out as you breathe in. Create space for the breath of God as you pray. Concentrate on this breath that sustains life and supports you as you connect to your source.

- Use this as a morning prayer outdoors, or as a walking meditation.

- The practice of Pranayama (a Yogic breathing practice) promotes a calm, balanced, and focused mind, and increases vitality and longevity. Try practicing morning Pranayama using this prayer.

Tradition/Path: Christian

Thought of Thee

*F*ather in Heaven!

When the thought of Thee wakes in our hearts

Let it not awaken like a frightened bird that

Flies about in dismay,

But like a child

Waking from its sleep

With a heavenly smile!

Origin:

Søren Kierkegaard (1813–1855), a Danish existential philosopher.

Options:

- Say this prayer upon awakening or upon retiring, reflecting on what the thought of God is for you, whether it brings a heavenly smile.

- You may change the greeting to "Mother in Heaven."

- Close the prayer with Amen, Blessed Be, or Shanti, Shanti, Shanti (peace, peace, peace).

Womb of All Creation

*I*nhabiter of Dark and Light,

You take us once more into yourself,

The womb of all creation,

Where nothing is understood

But all is known.

Reveal to us the wholeness

Promised in Christ before all time;

That, rooted in the soil

Of your unconditional love,

We go forth to proclaim with joy

The gospel of his coming;

Evening star,

Rising sun,

Energy that Shimmers throughout Time.

Amen.

Origin:

Mary Kathleen Speegle Schmitt, a contemporary Anglican priest and author of *Seasons of the Feminine Divine.*

Options:

- Examine your image of God. Has it evolved? Is it one-dimensional? Is it masculine? Imagine God as female as you read this prayer, as a mother or some other type of nurturing woman.

- Repeat one of the italicized images of the Creator and keep this in mind as you read the prayer again. Hold this image throughout the day.

- Change the closing to Ho (Native American), Blessed Be (Feminist), or Namaste (Sanskrit/Hindu).

Blessed art Thou, O Lord our God, Creator of the Universe, who brings forth bread from the Earth.

Jewish Blessing

Tradition/Path: Christian

Give Me Inward Vision

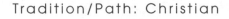

O Thou,

Who hast given me eyes

To see the light

That fills my room,

Give me the inward vision

To behold Thee in this place.

O Thou,

Who hast made me to feel

The morning wind upon my limbs,
    help me to feel Thy Presence

As I bow in worship of Thee.

Origin:

Dr. Chandran Devanesan, author, historian, and first Indian principal of the Madras Christian College in India.

Options:

- To encourage inward vision, pray with your eyes closed and try a different position for prayer than your usual stance. Alternate kneeling and prostration, for example, or pray while standing.

- Light a candle and do some candle flame meditation (see Down on Our Knees, Up on Our Toes, pp. 17–18) before and after the prayer.

Tradition/Path: Christian

I Rise Today

I rise today through

God's strength to pilot me,

God's eye to look before me,

God's ear to hear me,

God's word to speak for me,

God's hand to guard me,

God's way to lie before me,

God's shield to protect me,

God's hosts to save me

From the snares of the devil,

From everyone who desires me ill

From afar or near, alone or in a crowd.

Origin:

Saint Patrick (ca. 387–461). He developed a deep prayer life after being kidnapped by pirates and taken to pagan Ireland where he was sold as a slave to herd sheep. Later as a missionary bishop, he was instrumental in organizing the church in Ireland.

Options:

• Tune in to the heartbeat of God or the Great Mother. Imagine your heart beating in unison with your creator as you mindfully recite these words.

• Use this in addition to, or instead of, your usual morning prayer(s).

Tradition/Path: Anglican/Episcopal Christian

Alternative Lord's Prayer

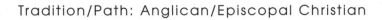

Eternal Spirit,

Earth-maker, Pain-bearer, Life-giver,

Source of all that is and that shall be,

Father and Mother of us all,

Loving God, in whom is heaven:

The hallowing of your name echoes through the
universe!

The way of your justice be followed by the
peoples of the earth!

Your heavenly will be done by all created beings!

Your commonwealth of peace and freedom
sustain our hope and come on earth.

With the bread we need for today, feed us.

In the hurts we absorb from one another, forgive
us.

In times of temptation and test, strengthen us.

From trials too great to endure, spare us.

From the grip of all that is evil, free us.

For you reign in the glory of the power that is
love, now and forever.

Amen.

Origin:

The New Zealand Prayer Book of the Anglican Church. The prayer book combines the traditional prayers and forms of worship of the Anglican Church (known as the Episcopal Church in America) with the earth-based spirituality of the Maori tribe of New Zealand and other Pacific island cultures.

Options:

● Use this prayer in place of the Our Father or a similar daily or morning prayer.

● Consider bracketing your day with this prayer by saying it in the morning and in the evening.

If you believe, you will receive whatever you ask for in prayer.

Matthew 21:22

Tradition/Path: Catholic Christian

Lead, Kindly Light

Lead, kindly Light,

Amid the circling gloom,

   Lead Thou me on,

The night is dark and I am far from home,

   Lead Thou me on,

Keep Thou my feet; I do not ask to see

The distant scene; one step's enough for me.

Origin:

Cardinal John Henry Newman (1801–1890) was a philosopher, Catholic apologist, and poet, as well as leader of the Tractarian Movement (Oxford Movement) of the nineteenth century. He is best remembered for his *Apologia*.

Options:

- Use "Lead, Kindly Light" in difficult times, times of decision, or before a trip.

- Read this prayer aloud to bring the words and message alive.

- Light a candle as you read the words, "Lead, kindly Light." Speak the words of the prayer into the candle's flame.

Tradition/Path: Christian

Evening Prayer

Lord of the Springtime,

Father of flower, field, and fruit

Smile on us in these earnest days

When the work is heavy and the toil worrisome;

Lift up our hearts, O God, to the things
    worthwhile;

Sunshine and night, the dripping rain,

The song of birds, books and music,

The voices of our friends.

Lift up our hearts to these this night, O *Father*,

And grant us thy peace.

Amen.

Origin:

Written by the educator/activist/writer W. E. B. Du Bois (1868–1963) around 1910, about the time he helped to establish the National Association for the Advancement of Colored People (NAACP). Although an agnostic, Du Bois found inspiration in the themes of the Old Testament.

Options:

- Make the language more inclusive by changing the italicized greetings to "Mother" and "Lady."

- Instead of or in addition to Amen, consider closing the prayer with Svaha (Amen in Sanskrit).

- Pause after the line "voices of our friends" to list specific friends and gifts in your life for which you are especially grateful.

When you pray, you open yourself to the influence of the power which has revealed itself as love. The power gives you freedom and independence. Once touched by this power, you are no longer swayed back and forth by the countless opinions, ideas and feelings which flow through you. You have found a center for your life that gives you a creative distance so that everything you see, hear and feel can be tested against the source.

Henri J.M. Nouwen

Tradition/Path: Taoism

The Ten Thousand Things

The Tao begot one.

One begot two.

Two begot three.

And three begot the ten thousand things.

The ten thousand things carry yin and embrace yang.

They achieve harmony by combining these forces.

Origin:

Lao Tzu, Chinese philosopher and an older contemporary of Confucius (fourth century) who is credited with writing the Tao te Ching. *Tao* means "the way ahead" and Taoism is based on the principle of action through inaction.

yin and yang

Options:

- Read this prayer facing yourself in a mirror. Repeat it until the words are stored in your memory.

- Be mindful of the elements of yin (female/lunar) and yang (male/solar) in your life today.

Tradition/Path: Hinduism

Beyond Darkness

In the early morning I bow to *Him*

Who is beyond darkness,

Who is like the sun,

Who is perfect, ancient,

Called Purushottama, the best among *men*

And in whom, through the veil of darkness,

We fancy the whole universe as appearing,

Even as, in darkness,

We imagine a rope to be a snake.

Origin:

Mohandas Gandhi (1869–1948) was the spiritual leader of the nonviolent civil rights movement to gain India's independence from Britain in the 1940s. Gandhi was called "Mahatma" which means "great soul."

Options:

- In Hinduism, Purushottama is invoked as an incarnation of Vishnu, one of the great Gods of Hinduism, worshiped as the Supreme by many. You may substitute the higher power of your choice.

- To make this prayer inclusive, change words such as "Him" to "Her" or "Purushottama" to "the Holy One."

Tradition/Path: Native American

Thanks to the Great Spirit

Now is the season of growing things;

Now we give thanks to our Creator, the Great
Ruler, the Great Life, the Great Spirit;

Now He listens to the words of the people here
assembled.

We give thanks for the return of the planting
season.

We give thanks again that we are permitted to take
part in this ceremony.

We give thanks for the earth Our Mother, from
whose breast all things grow.

We give thanks to Him for the seed to give back
to our mother.

We give thanks for rivers and waters that flow,

For herbs and plants and all fruit-bearing trees and
bushes that grow.

We give thanks that our supporters of life—corn,
beans, and squash, fail us not.

That famine is not permitted to enter our lodge
doors.

Origin:

Adapted from an Iroquois prayer.

Options:

- Native Americans burn dried tobacco, sweet grass, sage, and cedar in an open fire in a ceremony called smudging. The scented smoke carries prayers to heaven. If you would like to try smudging, look for good quality sacred herbs used in this ritual. They can be purchased through fine incense and candle suppliers and from Native American-owned stores in your area or online.

- Pray this prayer in the spring and the fall to remember the cycle of birth, growth, and death that is a part of all life.

- Read this prayer outdoors while you walk. Try to be conscious of nature's life-supporting bounty. Bring back a symbol of this bounty (a leaf, stone, or wildflower) for your prayer place.

Tradition/Path: Transdenominational

Blessing This Day

I only want to see the day ahead,

My attention will not go backward into my history,

And my attention will not go forward into my future.

I am committed to staying only in the present time,

To remaining grounded in my world,

To feeling a bond with each person I meet,

To respecting my own integrity and my own honor,

To living within the energy of love and compassion this day,

And returning to that energy when I don't feel it,

To making wise and blessed choices with my will,

To maintaining perceptions of wisdom and non-judgment,

To release the need to know why things happen the way they do,

And to not project expectations over how I want this day to be—

And how I want others to be.

And finally, my last prayer to trust the Divine.

With that I bless my day with gratitude and love.

Origin:

Caroline Myss is a medical intuitive and the author of numerous books, videos, and audios including *Why People Don't Heal and How They Can* and *Anatomy of the Spirit.*

Options:

- As you make an intention to live in the present tense today, focus on your seventh chakra, called the center of your truth and located at the crown of the head, which connects directly to spiritual guidance. Myss suggests that as you move through your day, you remind yourself that your spirit knows only the now. As you travel to work, sit and converse with a friend, enjoy lunch, tell yourself: This is all I have, this is all there is to my life, this is the present moment. Appreciate everything there is to the moment.

- The seventh chakra, also known as the crown chakra, is located at the crown of the head, the location of our "soft spot" as an infant. Touch your seventh chakra with holy water, or water that you have prayerfully collected, as you end this prayer with the alternative blessing: "I bless my day with gratitude and love."

Tradition/Path: Hinduism

Not This, Not That

In the early morning I worship Him

Who is beyond the reach

Of thought and speech,

And yet by whose grace all speech is possible.

I worship Him whom the Vedas describe

As neti, neti—not this, not that.

Him, they, the sages, have called

God of Gods, the unborn,

The unfallen, the source of all.

Origin:

Mohandas Gandhi, who refers here to the Vedas, the sacred scripture of Hinduism, perhaps the oldest books in the library of man, which represent the spiritual experiences of the Rishis, enlightened persons with a direct intuitive perception of Brahman, or the truth.

Options:

- Change the italicized gender terms to "Her."

- Use "Not This, Not That" as a morning prayer and reflect on "the source of all."

- Create a mandala to release your inner understanding of this invocation. Draw freely, reflecting on Him or Her who is "not this, not that."

For Today

O God:

Give me strength to live another day;

Let me not turn coward before its difficulties;

Let me not lose faith in other people;

Keep me sweet and sound of heart,

In spite of ingratitude, treachery, or meanness;

Preserve me from minding little stings or giving them;

Help me to keep my heart clean,

And so to live so honestly and fearlessly

That no outward failure can dishearten me or take away the joy of conscious integrity;

Open wide the eyes of my soul that I may see good in all things;

Grant me this day some new vision of thy truth;

Inspire me with the spirit of joy and gladness;

And make me the cup of strength to suffering souls;

In the name of the strong Deliverer,

Our only Lord and Savior, Jesus Christ.

Origin:

The Book of Common Prayer has been used since the mid-1500s by the worldwide Anglican Communion, which includes the Episcopal Church, USA, and the Church of England.

Options:

- If finding time to pray in the morning is difficult, keep this prayer on your night table and pray it before leaving bed; or leave the prayer taped to your medicine cabinet door so you will be reminded to make "For Today" a pre-tooth-brushing ritual.

- For a non-theistic version, omit the italicized passages or substitute your own.

- Choose one intention (e.g., "Preserve me from minding little stings or giving them") as your focus for the day. At evening prayers, reflect on how well you have honored this intention. Keep a journal if you like to record your spiritual progress.

- Close with Om, Ho, or Amen.

Tradition/Path: African

Mighty Force

*F*ather, O Mighty force,

That force which is in everything,

Come down between us, fill us,

Until we be like Thee

Until we be like Thee.

Origin:

Unknown author, New Guinea.

Options:

- Change the salutation of this prayer to "Mother, O Gentle Force."

- Change "between us" to "among us," mentioning those family and friends you hold in your heart.

- Use the italicized passage, "Until we be like Thee," as a mantra, repeating it throughout the day.

Tradition/Path: Christian Science

Thy Kingdom Come

Thy Kingdom come;

Let the reign of Divine Truth, Life, and Love

Be established in me

And rule out of me all sin;

And may thy word enrich the affections

Of all mankind and govern them.

Origin:

Mary Baker Eddy (1821–1910), the founder of the Church of Christ, Scientist (Christian Science) and author of the spiritual classic *Science and Health*. She believed that there was a "science" behind Jesus' healing method, and that it was "divinely natural and repeatable."

Options:

- Try using "Thy Kingdom Come" as an alternative to the Lord's Prayer.

- This prayer can be used before or after what Catholics call an "examination of conscience." At the end of the day, take a moment to look over your thoughts, words, and actions. Consider your intentions in each case. How can you go into tomorrow with better, more peace-full intentions?

Tradition/Path: Nondenominational

Stand by Us

Stand by us, O Awakener, as we arise

To each new morn.

Counsel us, O Guide, as we offer ourselves

In thy service.

Accompany us, O Unifier, as we face

Today's challenges.

Calm us, O Serene One, when worldly ways

Ignite temptation.

Companion us, O Friend, as we play

In the Dance of Life

And when this life journey is complete,

O Beloved,

Hie us Home to your Heart.

Amen.

Origin:

Nan C. Merrill, contemporary American author and editor of the *Friends of Silence* newsletter in Jericho, Utah.

Options:

- Try this as a "progressive "prayer, reciting lines 1–4 in the morning, lines 5–8 in the afternoon, and lines 9–13 in the evening.

- Close your eyes, sit in silence, and meditate on this reflection.

- Consider the various names for God listed in the prayer. Can you add others of your own?

If you want to pray, you are already praying.

The Desert Fathers

That I Might. . . .

Oh, that I might ever know

    Your Presence in every face

    Your Pulse in every heart;

That I might ever feel

    Your Breath in every breeze

    Your Touch in every rain drop;

That I might ever see

    Your Smile in every bloom

    Your Might in each sunrise.

And oh, please grant

That I might view

    Life's beauty through

    Your Eyes.

Origin:

Lynn L. Salata, contemporary American author. Taken from *The Beams of Prayer* by Edward J. Farrell, compiled and edited by Lynn L. Salata.

Options:

- Try listening to chant (Christian, Buddhist, etc.) to help you center before devotions.

- Use this prayer during the day when you break for devotions, repeating it on rising, at noon or lunch, and upon retiring.

- Today, make the effort to see God's presence in every face you meet. Note the experience in your prayer journal.

Tradition/Path: Christian

Bedtime Prayer

God, save us

God hide us.

When we sleep, God do not sleep.

If we sleep, God do not get drowsy.

Origin:

Unknown

Options:

- You may change the language to reflect the higher power(s) you reverence.

- Teach this to and say it with your smallest child or children at bedtime.

Tradition/Path: Buddhism

Waking Up

W aking up this morning I smile,

Twenty-four brand new hours are before me.

I vow to live fully in each moment

And to look at all beings with eyes of
compassion.

Origin:

Composed by the Buddhist teacher, activist, and author Thich Nhat Hanh. Originally from Vietnam, in 1982 he founded the International Buddhist Practice Center, called Plum Village, in France.

Options:

- Keep this vow on the mirror of your medicine cabinet or the door of the refrigerator so you will be reminded to repeat it before leaving the house each day.

- Keep a copy of this prayer taped to the sun visor of your car to use as a "devotion in motion" when you begin your morning or evening commute.

- Use the italicized passages as a moving mantra to say throughout the day, or use for a seated meditation whenever you have ten free minutes.

The Anyway Affirmation

People are unreasonable,

Illogical and self-centered.

I will love them anyway.

If you do good, people will accuse you of selfish,
   ulterior motives.

I will do good anyway.

If you are successful, you win false friends and
   true enemies.

I will succeed anyway.

The good you do will be forgotten tomorrow.

I will do good anyway.

Honesty and frankness will make you vulnerable

I will be honest and frank anyway.

People who really need help

May attack you if you help them.

I will help them anyway.

If you give the world the best you have,

You may be punished.

I will give the world the best I've got anyway.

Origin:

Adapted from a sign on the wall of Shishu Bhavan, a home for abandoned babies in India established by Mother Teresa.

Options:

- Use this as a morning prayer, or pray it as an affirmation to begin a new work week; say it any time you need spiritual reinforcement.

- Recite this affirmation in the evening; add it to your evening prayers at day's end.

- Say "The Anyway Affirmation" while doing an evening seated meditation; light a mood-lifting scented candle or incense such as lemon verbena or hibiscus to enjoy while you meditate.

- For a faith-based version of the prayer, add "In Christ's name" after each affirmation, or "In the Name of Holy Wisdom," "In the Name of Divine Mother," etc.

> At the heart of silence is prayer. At the heart of prayer is faith. At the heart of faith is life. At the heart of life is service.
>
> Mother Teresa

Friendship

May we forge a new friendship with the natural
world

And discover a new affinity with beauty, with life,

And with the *Cosmic Christ* in whom all things
were created in heaven

And on earth, visible or invisible,

Whether thrones or dominions,

Or principalities or authorities. . . .

For all things were created through *Him* and for
Him

In *His* name.

Amen.

Origin:

Anonymous, from a Chinook Psalter.

Options:

- Use "Friendship" as a walking meditation outside in
  the natural world, or if you are indoors, say this prayer
  while using an object from nature as a devotional focus,
  for example, a seashell, branch, wildflower, pebble, leaf,
  or a fallen bird feather.

- Meditate upon one blessing in the natural world for
  which you are especially thankful each time you say
  this prayer.

- Replace the *italicized* salutations with a non-deist *salutation* if you prefer, e.g., Great Spirit.

- In place of Amen, close with the Native American Ho or Spiritus Sanctus.

O Lord, give me strength that the whole world look to me with the eyes of a friend. Let us ever examine each other with the eyes of a friend.

Ayurveda

Prayers
for Healing and Hope

Tradition/Path: Christian

With You

· ·

In me there is darkness,

But with you there is light;

I am lonely, but you do not leave me;

I am feeble in heart, but with you there is help;

I am restless but with you there is peace. . . .

Origin:

Dietrich Bonhoeffer (1906–1945), written while awaiting execution in a Nazi concentration camp at Flossenbürg, Germany.

Options:

- Use "With You" as an evening prayer, lighting a candle to acknowledge God's light.

- Say this prayer on a rosary, repeating the five lines until you have finished five decades. Add the arrow prayer, "May Peace Prevail on Earth," between each decade.

Tradition/Path: Nondenominational

Attitude of Gratitude

Faithful Creator,

You are the source and resource of all purposed and created life.

In an attitude of gratitude I accept your forgiveness and grace to forgive myself.

I accept your encouragement to learn what it means to be authentically human and make peace with my own humanity,

So that I can accept the sacredness of other beings.

With thanksgiving, I accept the spiritual, ethical, and moral responsibility for my own inner healing and joy.

I embrace the mystery of healthy loving relationships

As I learn to be an agent of change, reason, and tenderness upon the earth

That is an outpouring of your love for all life.

I accept your help so that I may learn to live honorably in covenant community,

Lifting my voice in care over criticism.

Origin:

Adei-Mai Morningstar Grenpastures.

Options:

- Change this prayer from singular to plural ("I" to "we," etc.) to use it as an opening prayer for large meetings or gatherings.

- Try using this prayer for a labyrinth meditation. You may use a finger labyrinth if a full-sized one is not available to you. Read the prayer one line at a time, pausing at each turn of the path to read the next one. Walk meditatively, repeating the line silently or aloud. Alternately, read one or two lines, walk for a few minutes, pause to read the next few lines, and continue walking and reading. You may wish to close your prayer period with a few words from your own heart.

Tradition/Path: Nondenominational

Gently as Doves

Great Ideas, come into the world

As gently as doves.

Perhaps then *if I listen attentively,*

I shall hear amid the uproar

Of empires and nations,

A faint flutter of wings,

A gentle stirring of life and hope.

Origin:

Adapted from the journals of Albert Camus (1913–1960), a French novelist, playwright, and philosopher.

Options:

- Keep an origami or cloth dove on your altar to remind you of this prayer and all it symbolizes.

- Use the italicized words for *lectio divina.*

- Practice attentive listening. Sit in silence three times today. See what "gentle stirrings" you can identify.

All a Circle

We are all a circle.

Our dreams and prayers are at their core.

The same dreams and prayers

Our circle will lead out into the world,

And spread harmony over all the earth.

To remind us of this circle,

We envision one knot.

This knot will bind us together

In higher circles,

Each of us responsible for

One other person's prayer,

Responsible for other persons' prayers,

And the prayer that our circle represents.

We offer our knots up to the Great Spirit.

We are now separate,

And we are now joined.

May our prayers be as one.

May our unique spirits thrive

Independently and together. Ho!

Origin:

Lynn V. Andrews is an author and the founder of the Lynn Andrews Center for Sacred Arts and Training (www.lynnandrews.com).

Options:

- If you pray as a family or a group, create a sacred circle. Joining hands, read the prayer out loud to stimulate the special energy of the circle.

- Create a mandala, with your loved ones at the center. Working outward, add more people (and animals) to your circle of concern.

- If you are praying alone, visualize those you wish to pray with, living and passed, and join hands with them in your imagination.

- Create a prayer chain by e-mail with friends around the country (or world) and say this prayer at a specific agreed-upon time each week to create a "prayer vibe."

Tibetan monks creating a sand mandala

Tradition/Path: Native American

Teach Me to Sing

Giver of Life, Creator of all that is lovely
Teach me to sing the words of your song.

I want to feel the music of living
And not fear the sad songs
But from them make new songs
Composed of both laughter and tears.

Teach me to dance to the sounds of your world
And your people
I want to move in rhythm with your plan.

Help me to follow your leading
To risk even falling
To rise and keep trying
Because you are leading the dance.

Origin:

Author unknown.

Options:

- Recite this prayer as a walking meditation outdoors; move mindfully through "the sounds of your world."

- Try singing this prayer or creating a dance for the words.

Tradition/Path: Native American

I Seek Strength

Let me walk in beauty

And make my eyes ever behold

The red and purple sunset.

Make my hands respect the things you have made,

And my ears sharp to hear your voice.

Make me wise so that I may understand

The things you have taught my people.

Let me learn the lessons you have hidden

In every leaf and rock.

I seek strength,

Not to be greater than my brother,

But to fight my greatest enemy:

Myself.

Make me always ready to come to you

With clean hands and straight eyes.

So when life fades

As a fading sunset

My spirit may come to you without shame.

Origin:

This prayer is believed to have been written in the 1700s by a Native American.

Options:

- Consider this prayer as a prelude to an evening examination of conscience, or as an "emptying" ritual at day's end to reflect on how you have conducted yourself throughout the day.

- Use "I Seek Strength" as a walking prayer in a natural setting like a nature preserve, a trail, field, woods, or even a backyard. After you have recited the prayer, take it with you as you walk mindfully.

Tradition/Path: Catholic Christian

The Right Road

O Lord God,

I have no idea where I am going,

I do not see the road ahead of me,

I cannot know for certain where it will end.

Nor do I really know myself.

And the fact that I think I am following your will

Does not mean that I am actually doing so.

But I believe that the desire to please you

Does in fact please you.

And I hope I have that desire in all that I am
doing.

. . . I will trust you always

Though I may seem to be lost

And in the shadow of death

I will not fear,

And you are ever with me,

And you will never leave me

To make my journey alone.

Origin:

Thomas Merton, the Catholic contemplative and author, composed this prayer as a young Trappist monk. It is reminiscent of the psalms in the Bible but is unusual for its plain, conversational tone.

Options:

- The italicized passages can be used as stand-alone mantras.

- Pray this as a devotion before a trip.

- Substitute the name of your patron saint or angel for the phrase "O Lord God."

> Pure love and prayer are learned in the hour when prayer has become impossible and your heart has turned to stone. . . .
>
> Thomas Merton

Tradition/Path: Christian Feminism

Womb of All

Womb of All,

In the midst of a failing world,

You draw us into community with You,

And one another.

Contain us with the faithfulness

Of your motherly-compassion.

That, nurtured by your care,

We mother all who are in need

Of groundedness in You.

Birth-giver of the earth and skies

And all that is,

You are the one Divinity, now and forever,

Amen.

Origin:

Mary Kathleen Speegle Schmitt, a contemporary Anglican priest and author of *Seasons of the Feminine Divine.*

Options:

- Use an alternative Amen such as Blessed Be or Svaha.

- Do you have female images at your altar or prayer corner to inspire you? Consider those who "mother all who are in need," such as deities, saints, or earth spirits. Educate yourself about one female goddess, saint from another tradition, ancestor, or feminine image of the almighty and add an icon, statue, photo, or other symbol in their honor to your sacred space.

Tradition/Path: Anglican/Episcopal Christian

Fear Not

Lord, purge our eyes to see

Within the seed a tree,

Within the glowing egg a bird

Within the shroud a butterfly

Till, taught by such we see

Beyond all creatures, thee

And harken to thy tender word

And hear its "Fear not; it is I."

Origin:

Christina Rossetti, pre-Rafaelite poet and Anglican, 1830–1894.

Options:

- Start your day with this prayer but also take it with you through the day. . . . Write the words "Beyond all creatures, thee" or "Fear not; it is I" on slips of paper and post them where you will see them at strategic points in your day and be reminded that God is before us, with us, within us.

- You can omit "Lord" to make this an affirmation of creation and substitute "Mighty Creation."

Tradition/Path: Christian

Breathe Into Me

Breathe into me, Holy Spirit,

That my mind may turn to what is holy.

Move me, Holy Spirit,

That I may do what is holy.

Strengthen me, Holy Spirit,

That I may preserve what is holy.

Protect me, Holy Spirit,

That I may never lose what is holy.

Origin:

Saint Augustine (354–430), who wrote about the psalms, the gospels, and the great doctrines of the church, but who is best remembered for the story of his spiritual journey, *Confessions*.

Options:

- Hildegard von Bingen defined prayer eight centuries ago as "breathing in and out the one breath of the universe." Imagine yourself involved in this spiritual respiration as you pray. Bring lightness to your devotions by thinking of yourself as Hildegard did as "a feather on the breath of God."

- Use the words "Holy Spirit" today as your mantra. Repeat them silently throughout the day, pausing to close your eyes and draw a deep holy breath from the universe.

Tradition/Path: Christian Feminism

One Whose Love Is Enough

One whose love is enough

And all that we can desire,

Your power is made perfect

In our vulnerability.

Continue to call us back to you

And to one another;

That, acknowledging You as the source

Of our strength and hope,

We claim the reality of your reign on earth.

Womangod,

Emanating love, power, and justice.

You are our Goddess Three-in-One.

Amen.

Origin:

Mary Kathleen Speegle Schmitt, a contemporary Anglican priest and author of *Seasons of the Feminine Divine.*

Options:

- See God in God's fullness. Include Feminist prayers in your daily canon, reflecting on the fact that the Aramaic word often translated as "kingdom" is related to the word for Great Mother, while the word we

translate as "daily bread" derives from the roots for Holy Wisdom or Sophia.

- Recite this prayer on a rosary or on your wrist mala, repeating the prayer as often as necessary.

mala beads

Tradition/Path: Catholic Christian

Holy Virtues

Hail, Queen Wisdom,
May the Lord protect you
With your Sister, holy pure Simplicity.
Lady holy Poverty,
May the Lord protect you
With Your Sister, holy Humility.
Lady holy Charity,
May the Lord protect you
With your Sister, holy Obedience.
O most holy Virtues,
May the Lord protect all of you
From Whom you come and proceed.
There is surely
No one in the whole world
Who can possess any one of you
Unless he dies first.
Whoever possesses one of you
And does not offend the others,
Possesses all.
Whoever offends one of you
Does not possess any
And offends all.
And each one destroys vices and sins.

Origin:

Saint Francis (ca. 1181–1226), founder of the Order of Friars Minor and the patron saint of animals and the environment. This prayer is from his *Salutation of the Virtues*.

Options:

- Express your humility and obedience by removing your shoes and bowing down several times on your prayer rug (if you have one).

- Make *gasho* (join your hands) as Buddhists do in prayerfulness.

Tradition/Path: Islam

Know Myself

I thank you Lord for knowing

Me better than I know myself,

And for letting me know myself

Better than others know me.

Make me, I ask you then, better

Than they suppose,

And forgive me for what they do not know.

Origin:

Abu Bakr (ca. 573–634), father-in-law of the prophet Muhammad. He was the first caliph (successor) of Muhammad and was instrumental in the spread of Islam as a world religion.

Options:

- The Bible says that God knew us before we were even born (Jeremiah 1:5). Who better then to show us our true selves? Take a moment during your busy day to see yourself as others see you. Do you like what they see?

- Use "Know Myself" at the end of the day as a prayer of confession, pausing to reflect on how you portray yourself to the world around you.

Be the Canoe

O Jesus,

Be the canoe that holds me in the sea of life.

Be the steer that keeps me straight.

Be the outrigger that supports me in times of
great temptation.

Let thy spirit be my sail that carries me through
the day.

Keep my body strong,

So that I can paddle steadfastly on,

In the long voyage of life.

Origin:

A New Hebridean prayer, author unknown.

Options:

- Use this prayer as a meditation before your daily
commute or before leaving on a trip.

- Keep a toy boat on your altar as a symbol of the
challenges of the spiritual passage.

Tradition/Path: Hinduism

Body and Soul

May there be voice in my mouth, breath in my
  nostrils,

Sight in my eyes, hearing in my ears;

May my hair not turn gray or my teeth purple;

May I have much strength in my arms.

May I have power in my thighs, swiftness in my
  legs,

Steadiness in my feet.

May all my limbs be uninjured and my soul
  remain unconquered.

Origin:

The Atharva Veda. Here, as in other parts of the Hindu
Vedas (Vedic code), physical well-being is sought
alongside spiritual and moral values.

Options:

- Make this prayer into a bookmark. It can be a mind-
  body-spirit marker in whatever you read (book,
  newspaper, magazine) while working out on a treadmill
  or exercise bike.

- Put God into the equation, if you like, by adding a
  salutation and an Amen (or alternative) in closing.

Tradition/Path: Catholic Christian

E n d o w   M e

O Lord, endow me with more contentedness in
   what is present,

And less solicitude about what is future;

With a patient mind to submit to any loss of what
   I have,

Or to any disappointment of what I expect.

Origin:

Bishop Simon Patrick, seventeenth-century composer
of hymns.

Options:

- Use this as an evening prayer, before or after a prayer
  of contrition or reconciliation

- Substitute the salutation of your choice for "O Lord,"
  or for a non-religious affirmation, omit "O Lord."

Tradition/Path: Islam

G u i d e U s

Guide us, O God the All-Knowing,

To acquire knowledge.

It enables the possessor to distinguish right from
 wrong;

It lights the way to heaven.

It is our friend in the desert,

Our society in solitude,

Our companion when friendless.

It guides us to happiness;

It sustains us in misery;

It is an ornament among friends and armor against
 enemies.

Origin:

Muhammad, born in what is present day Saudi Arabia
around 570 A.D., was a prophet, philosopher, orator,
apostle, legislator, and warrior.

Options:

- Close the prayer with Amen, Svaha, Shanti, etc.

- Open "Guide Us" with a blessing from the "Blessings"
  section of this book, or by lighting a candle as you
  pray.

- Catholics might wish to add Saint Thomas Aquinas,
  patron saint of knowledge, to this invocation.

Give Me Light

O *God, give me light in my heart*

And light in my tomb,

And light in my hearing and light in my sight,

And light in my feeling and light in all my body,

And light before me and light behind me,

And light on my right hand and light on my left hand,

And light above me and light beneath me.

O *Lord, increase light within me,*

And give me light, and illuminate me.

Origin:

Ali ibn Abu Talib, the fourth of the caliphs of Muhammad. Born in 600 A.D., he was revered for his wisdom and remembered for his writings collected in the *Sentences of Ali.*

Options:

- Using small votive candles, light one as you speak every other line, or light one candle as you speak the first line and a second as you close with "illuminate me."

- Use "Give Me Light" as a morning prayer and choose one line (consider one of the italicized passages) as the light you will carry within reflectively throughout the day extending to all you meet.

- Say this prayer on prayer beads, repeating the lines until you have completed the circuit of beads.

Tradition/Path: Interfaith

Great Spirit

Great Spirit,
Grant us eyes to see thee.
God in all things,
All things in God.
Concealed in the manger,
Embodied on the wood,
Revealed as the stranger
In Bethlehem's stable,
On Golgotha's tree,
At Emman's table,
Would we see thee.
Our host and our guest,
Born among the beasts
Our most and our best
Among us as our least.

Help me to go on doing good,
Protect us from all danger
And transform me as you would.

Origin:

Anonymous

Options:

- Use "Great Spirit" as a morning prayer and practice seeing "God in all things" this day, seeing the most and the best in all you meet.

- Make notes about the people you meet each day in your prayer journal. See how this focus changes your perceptions and habitual ways of seeing others.

- Seal the prayer with Alleluia or Blessed Be.

O Great Spirit, help me never to judge another until I have walked two weeks in his moccasins.

Unknown

Tradition/Path: Christian

God of the Past, Present, and Future

God of the past, help us to let go of the things that hold us in bondage: anger and resentment,

Lingering doubt and disappointment, guilt and failure,

And even the dusty laurels of some long gone success.

Help us to entrust our past to you so that we might be free to greet you,

Our God of the present.

Let us be alive to the opportunities of each moment and alert to the opportunities of this time we share today.

Help us to be awake so that we may savor all the fullness of life

As it unfolds right now.

And Holy God of the future, give us a vision of hope that we might see beyond

The worries and discouragement and problems of today,

That we may grasp the future that you are surely bringing to our lives

And our world.

Help us stretch our imaginations so that we may
be open to the changes

That your future makes possible.

In the shadow of your everlasting presence, we
pray.

Amen.

Origin:

The Rev. Dr. Ralph E. Ahlberg is Secretary of the
Board of Trustees of Hartford Seminary in Hartford,
Connecticut, and is the author of *Holy Granite on High
Ground.*

Options:

- Use this prayer daily, before and during any new
undertaking or life change or during a time of trial.

- Create a mandala to express your feelings about God's
place in your past, present, and future.

- To practice surrender, bow down or prostrate yourself
fully as you read the first line of each stanza.

Different Paths

You, the one

From whom on different paths

All of us have come.

To whom on different paths

All of us are going.

Make strong in our hearts what unites us;

Build bridges across all that divides us;

United make us rejoice in our diversity.

At one in our witness to your peace,

A rainbow of your glory.

Amen.

Origin:

Brother David Steindl-Rast, O.S.B., Mount Savior Monastery, New York.

Options:

- Path is key here. If you have a zen garden (tabletop sandbox), create your own path while you recite the words of this prayer, creating a "rainbow of glory" for the day to make strong in your heart what unites you to all others.

- As you take a midday walk, use this prayer as a focus on how you have been walking the path of diversity this day. Use whatever line speaks to you for *lectio divina* reflection.

- Instead of Amen close with Salaam, Om Shanti, or Praise Be.

Real prayer penetrates to the marrow of our soul and leaves nothing untouched. The prayer of the heart is prayer that does not allow us to limit our relationship with God to interesting words or pious emotion . . . the prayer of the heart is the prayer of truth.

Henri J.M. Nouwen

Tradition/Path: Judaism

May I Be Alone

Grant me the ability to be alone;

May it be my custom to go outdoors each day

Among the trees and grasses,

Among all growing things,

And there may I be alone,

To talk with the one that I belong to.

Origin:

Rabbi Nachman of Breslov (1772–1810), celebrated rabbinical teacher and mystic of Eastern Europe. He was the founder if Breslover Hasidism.

Options:

- Use as a part of your spring or summertime morning prayer ritual. If praying indoors, arrange a flower or leaf of the season on your altar or praying corner. Press the flower or leaf between two books until dry. Use your pressed flower or leaf as a marker for a missal or spiritual book.

- Try spending a day or morning completely alone—no television, radio, telephone, Internet—no outside contact. Read this prayer at the beginning and end of your Day (or half-day) of Silence.

You Know the Way

In me there is darkness,

But with you there is light;

I am lonely, but you do not leave me;

I am feeble in heart, but with you there is help;

I am restless, but with you there is peace.

In me there is bitterness, but with you there is
   patience;

I do not understand your ways,

But you know the way for me.

Origin:

Dietrich Bonhoeffer (1906–1945) was an author,
musician, and Lutheran minister. He was one of the
few Protestant Christians who opposed National
Socialism in Germany. He was also a leader of the anti-
Nazi Confessing Church and the Abwer resistance
circle, a small Protestant resistance movement. He
wrote this prayer while awaiting execution in a Nazi
prison for his role in the resistance.

Options:

- Say "You Know the Way" as a bedtime prayer. Light a
candle, perform an examination of conscience, then
blow out the candle and say this prayer. Follow this
with five or more minutes of meditation before
retiring.

- Use the italicized passage as a mantra throughout the day.

- Pray this prayer before walking a labyrinth or before finger-walking a tabletop labyrinth.

Tradition/Path: Taoism

See the Small

I will see the small and develop clear vision

I will practice yielding and develop strength

I will use the outer light to return to the Inner
  light

And save myself from harm.

Origin:

Adapted from Lao Tzu, author of the Tao te Ching.

Options:

- Use "See the Small" as a spoken or mental mantra throughout the day to refocus your energies on the tasks of the day.

- Try praying this prayer to gain peace while stuck in traffic or at a red light during your daily commute.

- Recite this prayer in the evening following your examination of conscience or reconciliation ritual.

Tradition/Path: Transdenominational

Strength to Surrender

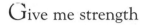

Give me strength

Never to disown the poor

Or bend my knees before insolent might,

Give me the strength to raise my mind

High above daily trials.

And give me the strength to surrender my strength

To Thy will with love.

Origin:

Rabindranath Tagore (1861–1941), one of modern India's greatest poets and Nobel laureate for literature in 1913, was also a freedom fighter and the author of independent India's national anthem.

Options:

- Say this prayer before or after making an examination of conscience at the end of the day.

- If you usually pray kneeling or seated, try praying in a prostrate position as an expression of surrender.

- You may wish to add a salutation and closing, naming your higher power.

Tradition/Path: Native American

Voice in the Winds

O Great Spirit,
Whose voice I hear in the winds
And whose breath gives life
To all the world,
Hear me! I am small and weak.
I need your strength and wisdom.
Let me walk in beauty
And make my eyes
Ever behold the sunset.
Make my hands respect the things
You have made.
And my ears sharp to hear your voice.
Make me wise
So that I may understand
The things you have taught my people.
Let me learn the lessons
You have hidden in every leaf and rock.
I seek strength,
Not to be greater than my brother,
But to fight my greatest enemy—myself.
Make me always ready to come to you
With clean hands and straight eyes.
So when life fades, as the fading sunset,
My spirit may come to you without shame.

Origin:

Unknown

Options:

- Add the Native American Ho or I Ask This for Myself, My People and All My Relations, or the Hindu Om Shanti in closing.

- Divide the prayer into three shorter prayers, starting with one of the italicized lines, and pray progressively through the day, at breakfast, lunch, and dinner.

- If you practice *lectio divina*, choose one of the italicized phrases to meditate upon after reading the prayer through.

Prayer from the heart can achieve what nothing else can in the world.

Mohandas Gandhi

Face to Face

··

O God, my master,

Should I gain the grace to see you face to face,

When life is ended,

Grant that a little dog, who once pretended

That I was God,

May see me face to face.

Origin:

Written by Francis Jammes (1868–1938), French poet and novelist.

Options:

- Recite this prayer at the end of day as an evening prayer or after your nightly examination of conscience and reconciliation.

- "Any object, stone, plant, can be placed in the center of a circle of mystery and regarded in its dimension of wonder, as a support for meditation," says Joseph Campbell. Place a small stuffed or china dog on your altar, or place of prayer, and use it as a support for meditation after you pray the above.

Prayers of Gratitude and Grace

Tradition/Path: Christian Feminism

For All Things

For all things bright and beautiful,

For all things dark and mysterious and lovely,

For all things green and growing and strong,

For all things weak and struggling to push life up
   through rocky earth,

For all human faces, hearts, minds, and hands

Which surround us,

And for all nonhuman minds and hearts, paws

And claws, fins and wings,

For this Life and the life of the world,

For all that you have laid before us, O God,

We lay our thankful hearts before you.

Origin:

Dr. Gail A. Ricciuti, Associate Professor of Homiletics
at Colgate Rochester Crozer Divinity School in
Rochester, New York.

Options:

- This prayer helps us develop compassion. Before praying each day, take a minute to locate your "feeling heart," or what Jesus called the heart shrine. Close your eyes and move out of your head and into your heart.

- After each line, think of an example of "for all things" that particularly moves you (for example, your garden, the hundred-year-old trees in your yard, or the herbs on your windowsill).

- Each time you read the italicized lines above lift up a different person so that the prayer becomes a living prayer chain.

Rising early the next morning, Jesus went off to a lonely place in the desert; there he was absorbed in prayer.

Mark 1:35

Tradition/Path: Nondenominational

Blessing

The blessing of God,

The eternal goodwill of God,

The shalom of God,

The wildness and the warmth of God,

Be among us and between us

Now and always.

Amen.

Origin:

Unknown

Options:

- Light a candle to mark the passing of the day's light while you say this prayer.

- This is a good time to review the day and give thanks for the gift of the last twenty-four hours. If you set an intention for the day, how well did you honor it?

Tradition/Path: Catholic Christian

Worthy to Serve

M ake us worthy, Lord

To serve our fellow men throughout the world

Who live and die in poverty and hunger.

Give them, through our hands, this day their daily
   bread,

And by our understanding love,

Give peace and joy.

Origin:

Mother Teresa, founder of the Missionaries of
Charity of Calcutta; she was beatified in 2004.

Options:

- Use this as a prayer before or after a meal.

- Think of ways to share your daily bread and bring this
  prayer to life. Can you feed leftover bread to the birds,
  donate packages of bread mix to the local food pantry,
  or bake bread for the local soup kitchen?

Prayer is the service of the heart.

The Talmud

Tradition/Path: Buddhism

Dharma

Assailed by afflictions, we discover Dharma

And find the way to liberation. Thank you, evil
forces.

When sorrows invade the mind, we discover
Dharma

And find lasting happiness. Thank you, sorrows!

Through harm caused by spirits we discover
Dharma

And find fearlessness. Thank you, ghosts and
demons!

Through people's hate we discover Dharma

And find benefits and happiness. Thank you,
those who hate us!

Through cruel adversity, we discover Dharma

And find the unchanging way. Thank you,
adversity!

Through being impelled by others, we discover
Dharma

And find the essential meaning. Thank you, all
who drive us on!

We dedicate our merit to you all, to repay your
kindness.

Origin:

Gyalwa Longchenpa, author of one of the classic Buddhist texts, *Thirty Pieces of Advice From the Heart*. *Dharma* is Sanskrit for "divine law."

Options:

- Use this prayer in the morning as your intention to practice gratitude for everything during the day as a way of observing your Dharma.

- Read through the prayer mindfully and find one line to use for *lectio divina*. Reflect on these words in silence, journaling if it is helpful to record your thoughts.

Tradition/Path: Buddhism

This Food

This food comes from the earth and the sky

It is the gift of the entire universe

And the fruit of much hard work

I vow to live a life that is worthy to receive it.

Origin:

A traditional Buddhist mealtime prayer.

Options:

- The Buddhist monk Thich Nhat Hanh tells us that looking at a simple piece of bread, we can see the sun, the rain, the earth, and the seeds that contributed to its creation. Many things in God's creation cooperated to produce this piece of bread, this meal for our nourishment. Pause to consider this vast interactive network before picking up fork or spoon. Pause to reflect that everything in life (including life itself) is a gift from the Creator.

- Recalling that giving thanks for the gift of food was humankind's first act of worship, resolve never to let a meal pass without quiet or spoken acknowledgment.

Tradition/Path: Islam

Unto His Light

Allah is the Light of the heavens and the earth.

His light is like a niche in which there is a lamp.

The lamp is in a glass.

The glass is, as it were, a shining star.

This lamp is kindled from a blessed tree, an olive,
  neither of the East or the West,

Whose oil would almost glow forth of itself,

Though no fire touched it.

Light upon light,

Allah guideth unto His light whom He will.

Origin:

The Holy Qur'an (or Koran), the sacred book of Islam, was revealed to the prophet Muhammad and established as a canonical text around 650. Qur'an means "reading" or "recitation."

Options:

- Substitute God, Creator, Great Mother, etc. for Allah.

- Light several small candles, one for each line in italics, as you read it. Pause to reflect. Read the prayer a second time, this time extinguishing each candle as you read the italicized line.

Tradition/Path: Christian

Before and After Meal Grace

Before

I was hungry;

And you gave me food.

I was thirsty;

And you gave me drink.

I was a stranger;

And you welcomed me.

I was naked and you clothed me.

I was ill;

And you cared for me.

Lord Jesus Christ,

May our hunger turn us toward our brothers

And sisters who are in need.

Origin:

Unknown

Options:

- If you are sharing the meal, let each diner read one line. At prayer's end, offer up the names of specific individuals or groups in need.

- You may omit "Lord Jesus Christ" and add your own higher power.

The Five Contemplations

· ·

This food is the gift of the whole universe—the earth, the sky, and much hard work.

May we live in a way that is worthy of this food.

May we transform our unskillful states of mind, especially that of greed.

May we eat only foods that nourish us and prevent illness.

May we accept this food for the realization of the way of understanding and love.

Origin:

This prayer is recited before every meal by Buddhist monks and nuns.

Options:

- Say this prayer as grace before or after meals.

- Carry this grace with you and read it prayerfully before you do your grocery shopping, to be more conscious of the experience.

  Follow this prayer with a few minutes of journaling, reflecting on one of the italicized passages.

Prayers of Contrition and Atonement

Tradition/Path: Christian

Fill Me With Perfection

O how scarce the number of souls who wish to
let the divine Creator

Work within them,

Who suffer in order not to suffer,

And die in order not to die!

How few are the souls that wish to deny
themselves,

To cleanse the heart of its longings,

Desires, satisfactions, of its self-love and
judgment!

How few who wish to follow the path of negation
and inner life!

Who wish to obscure themselves,

Dying to their senses and to themselves!

How few wish to vow, purify, and lay themselves
bare,

That God might dress them and fill them with
perfection!

Origin:

Miguel de Molinos (1640–1696), the founder of Quietism, a form of mystical asceticism (spiritual exercises in the pursuit of virtue) in the seventeenth century.

Options:

- Try a day or a half-day of silence, reading this prayer at designated times, such as rising, mid-morning, noon, mid-afternoon, and sunset. Couple it with a sitting meditation of ten minutes or longer.

- Recite this prayer before or after an examination of conscience.

Tradition/Path: Judaism

Day of Atonement Prayer

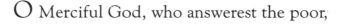

O Merciful God, who answerest the poor,

Answer us.

O Merciful God, who answerest the lowly in
spirit,

Answer us.

O Merciful God, who answerest the broken of
heart,

Answer us.

O Merciful God,

Answer us.

O Merciful God,

Have compassion.

O Merciful God,

Redeem.

O Merciful God,

Save.

O Merciful God, have pity on us,

Now,

Speedily,

And at a near time.

Origin:

A traditional Jewish prayer for the High Holy Days (also known as the Days of Awe) which includes the holidays of Rosh Hashanah and Yom Kippur. The Days of Awe are considered the most solemn period on the Jewish calendar.

Options:

- Pray in a group, family, or community. You may wish to share the reading of the prayer, passing a bowl of blessed water to each reader.

- If you are alone, read the prayer aloud (changing the "us" to "me") making a sign of the cross, or touching your forehead and heart with the water.

- You may wish to kneel, prostrating yourself after each line.

Kneel before you leap.

George H. Allen

Tradition/Path: Interfaith

Forgive Us Our Debts

Loose the cords of mistakes binding us,
As we release the strands we hold
Of others' guilt.
Forgive our hidden past, the secret shames
As we consistently forgive
What others hide.
Lighten our load of secret debts as
We relieve others of their
Need to repay.
Erase the inner marks our failures make,
Just as we scrub our hearts
Of others' faults.

Absorb our frustrated hopes and dreams,
As we embrace those of others
With emptiness.
Untangle the knots within
So that we can mend our hearts'
Simple ties to others.
Compost our inner, stolen fruit
As we forgive others the spoils of
Their trespassing.
Loose the cords of mistakes binding us,
As we release the strands we hold
Of others' guilt.

Origin:

A translation from the original Aramaic by Neil Douglas-Klotz of the line "And forgive us our debts, as we forgive our debtors" from the Our Father. What was translated from the Greek as "debts" or "offenses" can actually be understood as "hidden past," "secret debt," and "inner fruit."

Options:

- Add the salutation of your choice, such as O Lord, O Great Mystery, or Holy Mother. Try adding a different closing for the prayer each time you pray with it.

- "Forgive Us Our Debts" is a prayer for forgiveness. Choose a position of surrender (kneeling, bowing, or prostration) as you petition the higher power of your choice.

- Use this prayer as your act of contrition before bedtime. Pause to reflect on your spiritual day at the end of the prayer.

Tradition/Path: Hinduism

All My Wrongs

The wrong of ignorance,

The wrong of not having followed thee with a melting heart,

The wrong of not having meditated upon thee,

The wrong of not having prayed and worshipped thee,

O supreme Almighty, forgive me of all, all my wrongs!

Origin:

Pattinatar, a tenth-century Tamil saint.

Options:

- Open or close your reading with Ram, Ram, Ram (a Hindu invocation of God).

- Use this prayer as an evening act of reconciliation together with an examination of conscience.

Home At Last

O Gracious God,
Whose lover's quarrel with us
Is our anguish, history, and hope,
We confess that too often we lack courage
To join your lover's quarrel
With ourselves and the world.

We have not quarreled with power
When it's used for only the privilege of the few
Because too often we are the privileged.
We have not quarreled with the cleverness
That turns truth into lies that profit some
Because too often we've profited.
We have not quarreled with the arrogance
That dictates the domination of one race
Or nation, or gender or religion
Because too often we're the dominators.

Have mercy on us, heal us, Lord,
And deliver us from self-promotion,
Cowardice and lack of compassion.

Then empower us to be among those

Who dare to do things that are just and beautiful,

True and faithful, visionary and deeply joyful,

So that we may be free and whole

And home at last, home where we truly belong,

Home with our true selves,

Home with each other,

Home in the human family,

Home with you,

Through Christ Jesus,

Amen.

Origin:

The Rev. Dr. Theodore W. Loder was the Senior Minister of the First United Methodist Church of Germantown, Philadelphia, for almost forty years. Known for his involvement in social justice and civil rights issues, Dr. Loder is the author of numerous books, including *Guerrillas of Grace* and *The Haunt of Grace*.

Options:

- You may wish to change this prayer from plural to singular if you are praying solo.

- Break this prayer into three smaller prayers and use them upon rising (what Catholics call Prime), noon (called Sext), and at bedtime (called Compline).

Tradition/Path: Transdenominational

Full of Joy

O thou dweller in my heart,

Open it out, purify it, make it bright and
  beautiful,

Awaken it, prepare it, make it fearless,

Make it a blessing to others,

Rid it of laziness, free it from doubt,

Unite it with all, destroy its bondage,

Let thy peaceful music pervade all its works,

Make my heart fixed on thy holy lotus feet

And make it full of joy, full of joy, full of joy.

Origin:

Mohandas Gandhi (1869–1948) was the spiritual leader
of the nonviolent civil rights movement to gain India's
independence from Britain in the 1940s. Gandhi was
called "Mahatma" which means "great soul."

Options:

- Add the salutation of your choice (Dear Lord, Great
  Spirit, Universal Mother, etc.) and a closing (Amen,
  Shalom, Blessed Be, etc.) to make the prayer truly your
  own.

- If you pray with a partner, one of you can read one line
  while the other lights a tea light candle for each line; or
  you can take turns reading every other line.

- Say this prayer on a set of prayer beads, slowly
  repeating "full of joy" after each line.

Prayers for the Earth and the Animals

Tradition/Path: Indigenous

May the Earth

May the earth continue to live,

May the heavens above continue to live,

May the rains continue to dampen the land,

May the wet forests continue to grow,

Then the flowers shall bloom,

And we people shall live again.

Origin:

Anonymous author, from a collection of Hawaiian indigenous prayers of the people.

Options:

- To add the Creator to this prayer, alter each line from "the" to "your": "May your Earth . . . ," "May your heavens . . . , " etc.

- Use "May the Earth" to walk a full-sized labyrinth or to finger walk a tabletop labyrinth, letting each line trace one circle path.

- Pray this prayer as you walk in nature, adding a new line of your own making at the end each time you do so. You will have created an entirely new original prayer at the end of the spiritual year.

labyrinth in Chartres Cathedral, Paris, France

Tradition/Path: Nondenominational

Animals That Help Us

Father, we thank you for animals that help us,

For cows, sheep and horses;

Dogs that guard us and those that guide the blind.

We thank you, too, for all rare and strange
   animals,

And for those that make us laugh.

May we take care of them all.

Origin:

Unknown American author. It was thought to have
been written in the late 1800s.

Options:

- Make this prayer more personal by mentioning specific
  animals who have been companions in your life and in
  the lives of friends after each line.

- Fortify your prayer life by pausing for prayer five times
  a day in the Muslim tradition. Choose this prayer for
  the morning or evening and make other choices—
  prayers for people, for places, for the season, for
  nature—for the other four times you stop to meditate.

- Change the salutation, "Father," to reflect your
  spiritual tradition or path.

Tradition/Path: Indigenous

Ancient Sun

Ancient sun, eternally young

Giver of life and source of energy,

   In coal and oil, in plant and wind and tide,

   In spiritual light and human embrace,

You kindle the heavens, you shine within us,

(For we are sounds with hearts afire—

   We light the world as you light the sky

   And find clouds within whose shadows are dark),

We give thanks for your rays.

Origin:

Congregation of Abraxas, a Unitarian Universalist Order for Liturgical and Spiritual Renewal which existed from 1976–1985, drawing on many traditions, but especially from the Benedictine practice of the liturgical "Hours."

Options:

- Wake up early one morning. Pray this prayer while you watch the sunrise.

- Add a closing benediction that reflects your spiritual beliefs, such as Spiritus Sanctus or Om Mani Padme Hum.

- Add The World Peace Prayer Society's arrow prayer, "May Peace Prevail on Earth," as an Amen.

Tradition/Path: Anglican/Episcopal Christian

All Living Things

O God, you created all living things on the face of the earth

And gave us dominion over them;

Grant that we may be faithful to this trust in the way we treat all animals, both wild and tame.

Teach us to admire their beauty and to delight in their cunning;

To respect their strength and to wonder at their intelligence.

Grant that our use of them may be both merciful and wise.

So may we lend our voice to the praise of your goodness which endures forever.

Origin:

Charles Philip Price, Episcopal priest and professor. He was a major contributor to revisions of *The Book of Common Prayer* (1979) and the Episcopal *Hymnal* (1982).

Options:

- Choose one of God's creatures and study its life, habits, and psychology to gain a deeper understanding and appreciation of God's handiwork. Note what commonalities there are between all sentient beings.

- Find a way to do something merciful and wise for an animal this week.

Tradition/Path: Shinto

Nature's Shrines

There is no place
On this wide earth—
Be it the vast expanse of Oceans' waste,
Or peak of wildest mountain, sky-caressed—
In which the ever-present power divine
In every force of nature's not a shrine.

Origin:

Senge-Takazumi

Options:

- Is there a symbol of nature at your prayer place? If not, do an outdoor walking meditation and find one. Keep it on your altar or mat to be reminded of the Divine force in creation when you pray. Once a month, replace it with another of nature's gifts.

- Take time to praise the Holy One for this planet home. As the Sufi poet Rumi tells us, "Whoever feels himself walking on the path and refuses to praise . . . that man steals from others."

Tradition/Path: Celtic Christian

The Wind That Breathes

You are the wind that breathes upon the sea,

You are the wave on the ocean,

You are the murmur of leaves rustling,

You are the rays of the sun,

You are the beam of the moon and the stars,

You are the power of trees growing,

You are the bud breaking into blossom,

You are the movement of the salmon swimming,

You are the courage of the wild boar fighting,

You are the speed of the stag running,

You are the strength of the ox pulling the plough,

You are the size of the mighty oak tree,

You are the thoughts of all people,

Who praise your beauty and grace.

Origin:

Adapted from a traditional Celtic devotion, from the fifth or sixth century. Celtic tradition is a blend of Druidic spirituality with pre-monastic and early monastic Christianity in Britain and Ireland, producing prayers that are at once mystical and intensely earthy.

Options:

- If you have an altar or a special place where you pray, keep images or artifacts of nature that speak of divinity to you. Add objects from the changing seasons as a reminder of God's indwelling in all things.

- This devotion is ideally suited for recitation on prayer beads, one line to a bead. Even better, say your beads in the great outdoors, adding your own lines of praise as you walk or reflect.

Tradition/Path: Catholic Christian

Tapestry of Life

Creator God,

You make all things

And weave them together in an intricate tapestry
of life.

Teach us to respect the fragile balance of life and
to care for the gifts of your creation.

Guide by your wisdom those who have power and
authority,

That, by the decisions they make, life may be
cherished

And a good and fruitful earth may continue to
show your glory and sing your praises.

Almighty God,

You have called us to tend and keep the garden of
your creation.

*Give us wisdom and reverence for all your plants and
animals*

Who share this planet with us and whose lives
make possible our own.

Help us to remember that they too love the
sweetness of life.

And join us in giving you praise.

Origin:

The Eco-Justice Working Group of the National Council of Churches of Christ in the USA.

Options:

- If you live near a stream, pond, or river, you may wish to capture some water in a special bowl and pray a blessing on it. Keep this blessing bowl on your altar or at your prayer place and touch the water before and after this prayer.

- Keep a photo of your garden or a spot in nature you cherish on your altar. Or choose photos or drawings of plants or animals in your region which are endangered. Mention them by name during the prayer after the italicized line.

Migratory birds fly very high. . . . In that rarefied atmosphere they can fly very swiftly and easily. That is a parable of the way of prayer. Our souls are migratory souls. Our home is not here, but with God, to whom we seek to rise on the wings of prayer.

F. Andrew

Tradition/Path: Catholic Christian

The Web of Life

Good and Gracious God,
Source of all Life,
All creation is charged with your Divine Energy.

Ignite your spark within us,
That we may know ourselves
As truly human and holy,
Irrevocably part of the Web of Life.

All creation,
Each star and every flower,
Each drop of water and every person,
Each and every atom, down to its very electrons,
Explodes with the revelation
Of your Sacred Mystery.

May we always walk gently upon this earth,
In right relationship,
Nurtured by your love,
Taking only what we need,
Giving back to the earth in gratitude,
Sharing what we have,
Honoring all with reverence,
Reconciling and healing,
Mindful of those who will come after,
Recognizing our proper place as part of,
Not apart from, your creation.

Grant us the strength and courage, we pray,

For such radical transformation into your
Kingdom.

Then, we, too, with the very stones will shout
"Hosanna."

Origin:

Michelle Balek, OSF. Abridged from her "Prayer for Global Restoration" for Pax Christi USA. Pax Christi USA is a national Catholic peace movement that promotes nonviolence and social justice.

Options:

- Say this prayer outdoors as a presence within God's growing world, or in front of your altar bearing some gift from the earth (a rock, plant, leaf, or feather).

- Walk barefoot in the grass or sand after reciting this prayer, or close your eyes after reading and visualize a lush green outdoor scene where you are singing the Creator's praises.

- Choose an italicized passage to meditate on during the day in the context of your own life. (For example, "Sharing what we have": Am I generous in spirit in every instance? Do I give of myself in every encounter with others, or do I share after my own needs are met?)

Tradition/Path: Transdenominational

Oh Great Mystery

Oh Great Mystery

We give thanks for the natural world we see:

All the creatures, stones and plants

Who show us how to be.

We learn their lessons, seek their truths,

Return our loving praise,

We honor the peace they show us,

Which guides our human ways.

We ask that we may become like them,

Living in harmony,

And deep within our heart of hearts,

Know the Sacred Mystery.

Origin:

Jamie Sams, contemporary Native American writer and author of fourteen books.

Options:

- This is the perfect prayer to say anytime in God's backyard and/or as a walking meditation, reciting a line, walking and reflecting, reciting a second line, stopping to reflect, and so on.

- Say this prayer once daily for a week, using your journal to note the line of thought that speaks to you each day. Write about that thought in the context of your present life. Repeat this practice for the next six days, returning to the prayer at the end of this time and noting how your journal entries have changed your daily life.

prayer walking

Tradition/Path: Christian

She Who Is

Mother of dark soil,
    Morning star
    And vast ocean,
Mother who births plants,
    Winged creatures,
    Fishes,
    And four-footed beasts—
Mother who nurses the stars,
    The planets,
    The black universe—
Mother who suckles the children of earth—
Mother who holds creation in strong arms,
    Rocking it through the ages
    With the lullaby of life —
Show us your face, O Divine Mother.
Show us your face.

Origin:

Mary Lou Kownacki, OSB, is a feminist peace activist and the author of *Between Two Souls: Conversations With Ryokan* (Eerdmans, 2004).

Options:

- Can you invoke the Creator as Divine Mother? Shift away from all-male images for the Divine: add an icon, statue, or prayer card of a female deity or saint to your prayer place.

- Use the italicized passages as a focus for a walking meditation.

- Select a different symbol from nature—a rock, an ocean shell, a flower, etc.—as a focus each time you say the prayer.

Tradition/Path: Christian

The Measure of Love

Lord, may we love all your creation,

All the earth and every grain of sand in it.

May we love every leaf, every ray of your light.

May we love the animals; you have given them the rudiments of thought and joy untroubled;

Let us not harass them, let us not deprive them of their happiness, let us not work against your intent.

For we acknowledge that all is like an ocean, all is flowing and blending, and that to withhold any measure of love from anything in your universe is to withhold that same measure from you.

Origin:

Fyodor Dostoevsky (1821–1881). The great Russian writer was originally sentenced to death for his revolutionary activities but was later exiled to Siberia instead.

Options:

- You may substitute the name of your higher power in place of "Lord."

- Use "The Measure of Love" outdoors in good weather as a morning prayer, choosing one line as a mental mantra to carry with you for the day.

- Recite this prayer before or after you water your plants, feed the birds, or tend to your pets.

For the Entire Creation

I pray for the entire creation,

For the generation which is now alive,

For that which is just coming to life,

And for that which shall be hereafter.

And I pray for that sanctity which leads to
prosperity,

And which has long afforded shelter,

Which goes hand in hand with it,

Which joins it in its walk,

And of itself becoming its close companion as it
delivers forth its precepts,

Bearing every form of healing virtue which comes
to us.

And so, the greatest, and the best, and the most
beautiful benefits of sanctity

Fall likewise on our lot.

Origin:

This is a prayer of petition from the Zend-Avesta, the
scripture of Zoroastrianism, which is to be said upon
arising, to make sacred the day and all creation.

Options:

- Get in touch with the creation you are praying for: Go outside and pray while watching the sun rise. Remove your shoes and feel the earth, or pray lying in the grass.

- Open the windows or shutters, sit on a meditation cushion, and silently listen to the birds or creation's other sounds, after completing the prayer.

- Your chosen name for the Creator may be added at any point (for example, "I pray for the entire creation, Buddha," etc.).

meditation cushion

Prayers
for Peace and Justice

Tradition/Path: Christian Feminism

Heart of Compassion

Defender of Women and Children,

Out of pain and rejection

You molded Jesus' heart of compassion,

And caused Him to rise up

On behalf of outcasts and sinners.

Open our hearts to the despised

And rejected ones of the world;

That, surrounding them

With the intensity of your love,

We bring them into Your household

To be cherished by You forever;

Friend and Advocate of the Lost,

Liberating One.

Amen.

Origin:

Mary Kathleen Speegle Schmitt, a contemporary Anglican priest and author of *Seasons of the Feminine Divine*. This prayer is inspired by the belief that Jesus' position as a son of Mary rather than of Joseph in Jewish Palestine suggests that Jesus was perceived as illegitimate and suffered with Mary the rejection of society. His compassion for women and children may have stemmed from this experience.

Options:

- Can you open your heart to the "despised and rejected of the world"? Keep a photograph on your altar or at your prayer space of a starving child, homeless women and children, or victims of war and prejudice as a reminder of the daily need to develop our compassion and loving kindness.

- Consider sponsoring a needy child, or donating twenty dollars once a week (the cost of two pizzas!) to a local homeless shelter.

Send Thy Peace

Send Thy peace, O Lord, that we
May think and act harmoniously.

Send Thy peace, O Lord, that we
May be contented and thankful for
Thy bountiful gifts.

Send Thy peace, O Lord, that amidst
Our worldly strife, we may enjoy Thy bliss.

Send Thy bliss, O Lord, that our lives
May become a Divine vision and in Thy light,
All darkness may vanish.

Send Thy peace, O Lord, our Father and Mother,
That we Thy children on Earth may all
Unite in one family.

Origin:

Hazrat Pir-o-Murshid Inayat Khan (1882–1927),
founder of the Sufi Order in the West. His teaching
emphasized the fundamental oneness of all religions.
("Hazrat" is an honorific; "Pir-o-Murshid" is an
esoteric title signifying his position.)

Options:

- If you usually kneel, try sitting with your legs folded as for meditation. If you use a blessing bowl, bless yourself at the beginning of each line.

- Pray the five verses of this prayer on the five decades of a mala or rosary, returning to repeat the prayer if you choose.

- Light one candle (use small votive or tea light candles) as you say each verse.

Love All People

Eternal God, whose image lies in the hearts of all people,

We live among peoples whose ways are different from ours,

Whose faiths are foreign to us,

Whose tongues are unintelligible to us.

Help us to remember that you love all people with your great love,

That all religion is an attempt to respond to you,

That the yearnings of other hearts are much like our own and are known to you.

Help us to recognize you in the words of truth, the things of beauty,

The actions of love about us.

We pray through Christ, who is a stranger to no one land more than another,

And to every land no less than to another.

Origin:

World Council of Churches, Vancouver Assembly, 1983.

- Add an element of a faith that is foreign to you to your daily prayers. If you are Christian, read a passage from the Torah or the Qur'an. If your practice is Buddhist, listen to Christian chant instead of Hindu chant, or instead of your usual mantra say the Jesus prayer (Lord Jesus Christ, Son of God, have mercy on me, a sinner).

- Reflect on the idea that "the yearnings of other hearts are much like our own." Do you live this truth?

Hunger for Justice

O God,

To those who have hunger give bread;

And to those who have bread

Give the hunger for justice.

Origin:

Anonymous, Latin America.

Options:

- As you pray, lift up those persons, public figures, or organizations who need "bread" and those who need a "hunger for justice."

- Try chanting, rather than speaking or silently reading, this prayer. Chanting or singing creates vibrations and spiritual resonance which, according to Buddhist tradition, deepens the spiritual connection.

Tradition/Path: Nondenominational

Gather Us In

Gather us in, *Thou love that fillest all*;

Gather our rival faiths within thy fold.

Rend each man's temple-veil and bid it fall,

That we may know that Thou hast been of old;

    Gather us in.

Gather us in: we worship only Thee;

In varied names we stretch a common hand;

In diverse forms a common soul we see;

In many ships we seek one spirit-land;

    Gather us in.

Each sees one color of thy rainbow-light,

Each looks upon one tint and calls it heaven;

Thou are the fullness of our partial sight;

We are not perfect until we find the seven;

    Gather us in.

Origin:

George Matheson (1842–1906), Scottish theologian and preacher.

Options:

- Read each section, making the sign of the cross as you pray the line "Gather us in." (Note: Don't reject the sign of the cross if you are not a Christian. To the ancient Greeks, the four points of the cross represented the eternal elements: air, water, earth, and fire.)

- Choose one of the italicized lines to practice *lectio divina*. Carry the line with you throughout the day as a portable *lectio*.

Tradition/Path: Judaism

Shalom

May we drink deeply from the fountain of peace,
Know peace deeply in ourselves,
Live in peace with our neighbors,
Create peace in the world.
We bless the Holy One,
Creator of wholeness, Source of Peace.

May you guard my tongue from evil,
And my lips from speaking lies.
Help me ignore the taunts of my foes,
And to forgive those who wrong me.
Open my heart to the wisdom of the Torah,
So that my feet will follow the path of
    righteousness.

May all who study destruction have their designs
    frustrated,
May this happen for the sake of the holiness of
    the world.

May the words of my mouth
And the meditations of my heart
Remain true and loving
And be acceptable in your sight.

May your light show us the way

To bring peace to all.

Origin:

From *Siddur for Evening Shabbat* by Rabbi Marcia Prager. A siddur is a Jewish prayer book.

Options:

- Change "the Torah" to your personal sacred scripture as you read the line "Open my heart to the wisdom of the Torah."

- If you usually read the Christian Bible daily, switch to the scripture of another tradition one day a week. Try reading the Torah on the Jewish Sabbath, the Qur'an midweek, the Bhagavad Gita or Upanishads to start the week, or the writings of Confucius to inspire you for the weekend.

Tradition/Path: Hinduism

May There Be Peace

May there be peace in the higher regions;

May there be peace in the firmament;

May there be peace on earth.

May the waters flow peacefully;

May all the divine powers bring unto us peace.

The supreme Lord is peace.

May we all be in peace, peace, and only peace.

Origin:

The Vedas, the primary texts of Hinduism containing hymns, incantations, and rituals. There are four Vedas: the Rig Veda, Sama Veda, Yajur Veda, and Atharva Veda.

Options:

- Pray "May There Be Peace" using a rosary, adding your own personal wishes for peace.

- Recite this as a morning prayer, thinking about one personal way you can walk in peace this day.

- Choose one of the italicized lines, copy it on a small slip of paper, keep it in your pocket, and read it several times as a reminder of where you are sending your energies throughout the day.

Tradition/Path: Catholic Christian

Break Open Our Hearts

Spirit of Justice,
Break open our hearts. Break them wide open.
Let anger pour through
Like strong storms,
Cleansing us of complacency.
Let courage pour through
Like spring storms,
Flooding out fear.
Let zeal pour through
Like blazing summer sun,
Filling us with passion.
Force of justice, grant me
Anger at what is,
Courage to do what must be done,
Passion to break down the walls
Of injustice
And build a land flowing
With milk and honey
For God's beloved.
God's special love.
God's poor ones.

Spirit of Justice,
Break open our hearts.

Origin:

Mary Lou Kownacki, OSB, is a feminist peace activist and the author of *Between Two Souls: Conversations With Ryokan* (Eerdmans, 2004).

Options:

- Say this as a morning prayer, once a week. Choose a line or phrase for *lectio divina*.

- Record your daily reflections in your prayer journal. Review these insights at the end of six months or a year.

Tradition/Path: Transdenominational

Peace Is in Our Hands

Where there was no wine

There was you

And you said "drink,"

And there it was startling and sweet.

And where there was no bread

There was you

And you said "touch"

And there we were

Our hands looking like yours.

And where there is no peace

There is you

And you say "Lay down your arms"

And here we are

Holding one another

In loving embrace.

Peace is in our hands.

Origin:

Peace activist Jan Richardson.

Options:

- Use "Peace Is in Our Hands" as an evening prayer, as a prayer of gratitude at any time, or as a prayer before a meal.

- Say this prayer using a wrist mala, one line to a bead. Repeat "Peace is in our hands" after each sentence, saying the entire prayer several times.

- Add a closing like Shanti Shanti Shanti, Shalom, or Salaam to remind you that all religions desire peace.

Most people consider the course of events as natural and inevitable. They know little what radical changes are possible through prayer.

Paramahansa Yogananda

Prayers to the Saints, Angels, and Ancestors

Tradition/Path: Christian

This Earthly Fellowship

We thank you, God, for the saints of all ages;

For those who in times of darkness kept

    The lamp of faith burning;

For the great souls who saw visions of

    Larger truth and dared to declare it;

For the multitude of quiet and gracious souls

    Whose presence has purified and sanctified the world;

And for those known and loved by us,

    Who have passed from this earthly fellowship

    Into the fuller light of life with you.

Origin:

Unknown, third century.

Options:

- After reading the first line, mention your guardian angel or patron saint. You may wish to add the names of other holy persons who have been a lamp of faith for you after the corresponding line.

- At the end of the prayer, lift up the names of loved ones who have made the transition to "the fuller light of life." Then light a candle and keep it burning while you reflect.

Courage is fear that has said its prayers.

Dorothy Bernard

Tradition/Path: Transdenominational

For Making Me Possible

....

I honor you spirits

Help me find the wisdom to recognize the path
    and the courage

To follow it.

Help me find the courage to have faith.

Help me live within the great plan and fulfill it

By leaving the world better than it was given
    to me.

Thank you for making me possible.

Thank you for being my hosts.

Origin:

Composed by the author of *Keeping the Faith, in the
kiva, in New Mexico in 2001.*

Options:

- Pray "For Making Me Possible" outdoors on a starry
  evening.

- Add a salutation to the higher power to whom you are
  addressing this prayer, and close with Amen. Mention
  specific ancestors or saints by name after the line "I
  honor you spirits."

- Say each line of the prayer on its own prayer bead. Carry your prayer beads throughout the day, returning to the prayer and noting what different responses arise each time you pray it.

- Light a candle in front of pictures, icons, or symbols of your ancestors or saints during your prayer time.

icon

Mother in Faith

Mother in faith
Help us to cherish the old
And give birth to the new
As we strive to incarnate,
The Word in the World.

Sister in discipleship
Set forth to give and be gifted
Teach us to walk together
Ever ready to gift and receive.

Model of the Church
Show us how to be
Christ-bearers to the world as you were
At Cana—attentive to those in need
At Calvary—compassionate to all who suffer
At Pentecost—Spirit-filled and empowered.
Mother
   Sister
Model
With you we proclaim:
The time of rejoicing is here
God is among us!

Origin:

Unknown

Options:

- Consider electing one day a week as Mary's Day and beginning your day with this litany. Each week choose a different stanza to use for reflection throughout the day.

- Lift up other holy women of your tradition or from your life after the words "Mother," "Sister," and "Model."

Blessings

Tradition/Path: Celtic Christian

House Blessing

God bless the house from ground to stay,

From beam to wall and all the way,

From head to post, from ridge to clay,

From balk to roof-tree let it lay,

From found to top to every day

God bless both fore and aft, I pray,

Nor from the house God's blessing stray,

From top to toe the blessing go.

Origin:

Celtic Christians from North Uist, an island off the coast of Scotland. Written in the seventeenth century.

Options:

- We bless ourselves, our children, and our families, but we may forget to ask God's benediction of our dwelling place. Include this in your daily prayers. Include a photo of your home on your altar as a reminder of your blessings.

- Do the secular and the sacred meet in your life? For Celtic Christians there was no boundary between the two. Extend this domestic blessing today. How many gifts, major and miniscule, in your life can you identify and ask God's blessing upon today?

Tradition/Path: Transdenominational

Small Things

Dear Father,

Hear and bless Your beasts

And singing birds;

And guard with tenderness

Small things

That have no words.

Origin:

Unknown

Options:

- Recite this prayer in the outdoors, preferably where you can hear the birds or sounds of nature.

- Change the greeting to "Dear Mother," or a salutation reflecting your higher power.

- Form an intention to develop *agape* (unconditional love) toward all of creation, to grow in compassion and connectedness with all creation.

- Add the Amen alternative of Native Americans, I Ask This for Myself, My People, and All My Relations.

Tradition/Path: Native American

Our Father, the Sky

O our Father, the Sky, hear us.

And make us strong.

O our Mother, the Earth, hear us

And give us support.

O Spirit of the East,

Send us your wisdom.

O Spirit of the South,

May we tread your path of life.

O Spirit of the West,

May we always be ready for the long journey.

O Spirit of the North, purify us

With your cleansing winds.

Origin:

Anonymous Sioux Indian prayer.

Options:

- The Dakota Sioux have a simple centering practice: find a peaceful place, close your eyes, and imagine the light of God streaming down on you from the heavens. When you feel the warmth, say this prayer and send it heavenward.

- Close this prayer with the Native American Ho, or the Latin Kyrie Eleison.

Tradition/Path: Hinduism

Grant to Us Sight

May the sun guard us
In the highest heaven!
May the breezes protect us
In the airy spaces!
May fire be our guardian
In earthly places!
May the God of Light
Grant to us sight!
May God the Creator
Grant to us sight!

Give sight to our eyes
And sight to our bodies
That we may see.
May we see the world
At a single glance
And in all its details.
Thus, O Sun,
May we gaze on you,
Most fair to behold!
May we see clearly,
With the eyes of Men!

Origin:

From the Rig Veda, one of four Vedas. The Vedas are the primary texts of Hinduism. They contain hymns, incantations, and rituals.

Options:

- Add the words "Holy Mother" at the beginning and "Blessed Be" at the end of the prayer, or use alternatives to these greetings and closings.

- Punctuate this prayer by ringing a bell (or sounding a singing bowl) at the start of each line, pausing to reflect on the words.

The Water of Life

He who brought water is with us

He who brought bread is with us

We shall find the water

We shall be the water

I am the water of life

You are the water of life

We are the water of life

We shall find the water

We shall be the water.

Origin:

Dorothee Soelle, in *Revolutionary Patience*, a collection of prayer-poems. Soelle was a radical Christian Feminist theologian who wrote about issues from the Holocaust to Vietnam.

Options:

- Keep a copy of this prayer near sources of water in your home or in your gym bag with your water bottle.

- Use this as a prayer with groups at home, at church, or at the office.

- Keep a bowl of blessing water on your altar or at your prayer mat. Bless yourself as you begin and close this prayer.

Tradition/Path: Christian

Those I Love

God bless all those that I love;

God bless all those that love me;

God bless all those that love those that I love

And all those that love those that love me.

Origin:

This is an anonymous prayer said to have been stitched on a sampler by a young girl in Puritan New England.

Options:

- Carry this prayer with you in your wallet, briefcase, purse, or car to say in spare moments.

- Pray before an altar if you use one, gazing at a photograph of your loved ones, focusing on their faces for a few moments and repeating the prayer, sending loving energy out to each person.

- After each line, mention the specific names of people close to you whom you are lifting up in love.

Tradition/Path: Christian

Our Father, Mother

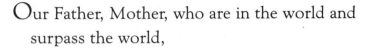

Our Father, Mother, who are in the world and
   surpass the world,

Blessed be your presence,

In us, in animals and flowers,

In still air and wind.

May justice and peace dwell among us, as you come
   to us.

Your will be our will;

You will that we be sisters and brothers,

As bread is bread, water is itself,

For our hunger, for quenching of thirst.

Forgive us.

We walk crookedly in the world,

Are perverse, and fail of our promise.

But we would be human,

If only you consent to stir up our hearts.

Amen.

Origin:

Daniel Berrigan, SJ, the contemporary Jesuit priest who is known for his antiwar and social justice activism (often with his late brother Phillip Berrigan).

Options:

- This may be used as a prayer upon rising, an alternative to the usual grace before meals, or whenever thanks or blessings are being offered.

- Add the World Peace Prayer Society's arrow prayer, "May Peace Prevail on Earth", in closing.

- The salutation and closing may be altered to reflect your spiritual tradition.

Tradition/Path: Nondenominational

No Easy Answers

May God bless me with discomfort at easy answers,

Half truths, and superficial relationships,

So that I may live deep within my heart.

And may God bless me with tears for those

Who suffer from pain, rejection and starvation, and
   war,

So that I may reach out my hand to comfort them.

And to turn their pain into joy.

Origin:

Anonymous, twentieth century.

Options:

- Use this as a morning prayer, at the start of meditation or the beginning of a retreat.

- Consider praying in a new, less comfortable position— try standing, bowing, or fully prostrating yourself.

- Use "No Easy Answers" with an evening examination of conscience.

Vows, Pledges, and Creeds

Tradition/Path: Nondenominational

One Great Family

Almighty God, who are mother and father to us all,

Look upon your planet Earth divided;

Help us to know that we are all your children,

That all nations belong to one great family,

And all of our religions lead to you.

Multiply our prayers in every land

Until the whole Earth becomes your congregation,

United in your love.

Sustain our vision of a peaceful future

And give us strength to work unceasingly

To make that vision real.

Amen.

Origin:

Helen Weaver

Options:

- If you pray the Hours (a Catholic tradition), use this prayer at Prime (6:00 a.m.) or Terce (9:00 a.m.). Use the italicized lines as a focus for a walking meditation at Sext (noon).

- Change this prayer from plural to singular (for example, "We" to "I") if you are praying alone.

- Try different openings and closings from different traditions each time you pray "One Great Family" to remind you that the religions of the world are all part of one congregation.

> Every Christian needs a half-hour of prayer each day, except when he is busy—then he needs an hour.
>
> Saint Francis de Sales

Tradition/Path: Buddhism

May I Be . . .

May no one who encounters me
Ever have an insignificant contact.
May the mere fact of our meeting
Contribute to the fulfillment of their wishes.

May I be a protector of the helpless,
A guide to those traveling the path,
A boat to those wishing to cross over,
Or a bridge or a raft.

May I be a lamp for those in darkness,
A home for the homeless,
And a servant to the world.

Origin:

Shantideva, eighth-century Buddhist spiritual master and mystic, known for his Sanskrit masterpiece *Bodhicaryavatara* (or *Guide to the Bodhisattva's Way of Life)*.

Options:

- A salutation (Dear God, Great Spirit, Mother of All, etc.) may be added to the prayer.

- Using a wrist mala, say a line while fingering each bead, repeating the prayer until you've finished your beads. Carry the mala and say the verses at key moments during the day to remind yourself of your vows.

Tradition/Path: Transdenominational

Ishwar Allah Abba-Ma

Abal-Adom-Tima

You are lovely,

Shy and gentle as a two-spotted deer

That weans the lonely forest

From the night.

I have been yours

Since I was born.

Every beat of my heart

Every breath of my mouth

Take as an act of love

And bind us all with you.

Origin:

An Indian Interfaith prayer created by John Shevlin, SVD, which harmonizes the six major world religions: AB—*Abba*, Christianity; AL—*Allah*, Islam; AD—*Adonai*, Judaism; OM—*Om*, Buddhism; TI—*Tien*, Confucian; MA— *Dharma*, Buddhist.

The title combines the Hindu word *Ishwar*, the Muslim word *Allah*, and adds *Abba-Ma*, a new Christian name for God that combines *Abba*, used by Jesus designating God the Father, and *Ma* for God the Mother.

Options:

- Use these ten lines to say a decade of your rosary, then repeat the prayer for as many decades as you choose. Pause for reflection and take ten minutes to journal, expressing the thoughts and feelings that arise.

- A salutation may be added (Dear God, My Creator, Mother Earth, etc.) after the italicized lines in the prayer.

Tradition/Path: Theosophy

One With Every Other

O hidden life, vibrant in every atom;

O hidden life, shining in every creature;

O hidden love, embracing all in oneness;

May all who feel themselves as one with thee,

Know they are therefore one with every other.

Origin:

Annie Besant, The Theosophical Society, a nonsectarian organization founded in 1875, seeking to reconcile religion, philosophy, and the science of the east and west.

Options:

- Use "One With Every Other" as a prayer for every new week, new month, or new moon.

- Use this prayer as a blessing upon any community activity, business meeting, or group activity.

Tradition/Path: Anglican/Episcopal Christian

Thy Will Be Done

Goodness is stronger

Than evil;

Love is stronger

Than hate;

Light is stronger

Than darkness;

Life is stronger

Than death;

Victory is ours

Through Him

Who loved us.

Origin:

Desmond Tutu, the South African anti-apartheid Anglican archbishop and Nobel Peace Prize recipient in 1984.

Options:

- Read this prayer in *lectio divina* fashion and choose the single line that speaks to you today. Carry this line with you during the day, pausing throughout the day to close your eyes and repeat it silently or aloud.

- Add the salutation of your choice to open the prayer (Blessed Mother, Oh Buddha, Jesu, etc.) and a closing such as Baptizus Sum or Ram, Ram, Ram.

Tradition/Path: Eastern Orthodox

Glory to Thee

O Father, my hope,

O son, my spirit,

O Holy Spirit, my protection.

Holy Trinity, glory to Thee.

Origin:

Saint Joannikios, archbishop and later patriarch of the Serbian Orthodox Church in the 1330s.

Options:

- Choose a line from the prayer such as "O Father, my hope" to use as a mantra for the day.

- If you pray the Hours or pause in the Muslim fashion to pray several times a day, use this prayer for one of those times.

- Make the sign of the cross (or touch your forehead and heart) as you read the words "Knowing how deeply." Or, speak the words in your heart as you strike a set of tingsha or a singing bowl.

tingsha

We Vow Not to . . .

Knowing how deeply our lives intertwine,

We vow not to kill.

Knowing how deeply our lives intertwine,

We vow not to take what is not given.

Knowing how deeply our lives intertwine,

We vow not to engage in abusive relationships.

Knowing how deeply our lives intertwine,

We vow not to speak falsely or deceptively.

Knowing how deeply our lives intertwine,

We vow not to harm self or others through

Poisonous thought or substance.

Knowing how deeply our lives intertwine,

We vow not to dwell on past errors.

Knowing how deeply our lives intertwine,

We vow not to speak of self separate from
others.

Knowing how deeply our lives intertwine,

We vow not to possess any thing or form of life
selfishly.

Knowing how deeply our lives intertwine,

We vow not to harbor ill will toward any plant, animal or

Human being.

Knowing how deeply our lives intertwine,

We vow not to abuse the great truth

Of the Three Great Treasures.

Origin:

Stephanie Kaza, professor of environmental studies at the University of Vermont and author of *The Attentive Heart: Conversations With Trees.* She practices the Zen Buddhist technique of *shikantaza*—just sitting—to find serenity and inspiration among trees.

Options:

- The Three Great Treasures are faith in the Buddha, faith in the Dharma (divine law), and faith in the Sangha (community). You may omit this line if you are not Buddhist, or you may add your own treasure here.

- If you say a morning creed, you may wish to substitute this prayer, or say it following your expression of faith, as an expression of ethical resolve.

Tradition/Path: Buddhism

Invocation

Let us invoke our ancestors,

Both spiritual and genetic,

For we are the sole reason for their existence.

Let us invoke the children,

And their children,

For they are the sole reason for our existence.

Let us invoke the mountains and rivers

And this great earth,

And acknowledge our intimacy

And interdependence

With all things sentient and insentient.

Let us reflect that the gift of life

Is more fragile than the dewdrops

On the tips of the morning grasses.

Then, let us vow.

Let us vow to heal and nourish.

Let us vow to love and share.

Let us vow to alleviate suffering and bondage.

Let us vow to manifest peace and joy

With wisdom and compassion.

May this century be known

To future generations as the beginning of

The Great Millennium of the Endless Spring.

Origin:

John Daido Loori, abbot of Zen Mountain Monastery, an American Zen Buddhist monastery and training center for male and female monastic and lay practitioners in the Mountains and Rivers Order. It is located in the Catskill Mountains in New York.

Options:

- You may omit the last three lines.

- Use this as a progressive prayer, praying a few lines in the morning, a few more at noon, and finishing the prayer in the evening.

- Pray this invocation on your prayer beads, reciting one line per bead.

Tradition/Path: Christian

I Arise Today

I arise today

Through the strength of heaven;

Light of sun,

Brilliance of moon,

Splendor of fire,

Speed of lightning,

Swiftness of wind,

Depth of sea,

Stability of earth,

Firmness of rock.

I arise today

Through a mighty strength, the invocation
   of the Trinity,

Through belief in the Threeness,

Through confession of the Oneness

Of the Creator of creation.

Origin:

Adapted from "The Breast-Plate of Saint Patrick," by
Saint Patrick, the patron saint of Ireland (and its
second bishop). He was born in Wales as Maewyn in
385 A.D. Because he used it to explain the Christian
Holy Trinity (Father, Son, and Holy Spirit), the

three-leafed shamrock is a symbol for his feast day on March 17.

Options:

- Create an altar with symbols of God's handiwork from nature, using some of the natural elements mentioned in the prayer. If you are a Christian, add a shamrock to the altar to symbolize the Trinity.

- Go outside to say this prayer, or stand near an open window. Failing that, bring the outdoors inside by listening to a recording of the sounds of the ocean, the rainforest, or wild birds.

- Use this as a walking prayer in a natural setting such as the woods, a field, or even your backyard.

Tradition/Path: Christian Feminism

God Who Dances

Ｍay the God who dances in creation,

And embraces us with human love,

Who shakes our lives like thunder,

Bless us and drive us out with power,

To fill the world with her justice.

Amen.

Origin:

Janet Morley, Vice President of the Evangelical Lutheran Church in Canada.

Options:

- Place both hands over your heart, opening them out as you read each line, to symbolize sending your heart energy into creation.

- Why kneel quietly in prayer when you can dance your prayer? Try creating a sacred dance to these words.

Tradition/Path: Buddhism

I Surrender

All the Buddhas in all the regions, I entreat with my
hands folded;

May they light the lamp of Dharma, for those lost in
suffering's wastes.

With folded hands I now petition the spiritual beings
[the *Bodhisattvas*]

Who are ready for Nirvana

To stay here still for many ages,

So that the world may not be struck with blindness.

Heedless of body, heedless of goods,

Of the merit I have gained and will gain still,

I surrender my all to promote the welfare of others.

Origin:

Santideva (ca. 70 A.D.), writing in *The Path of Light*.
Santideva was a Bengal prince who renounced his
position to seek enlightenment, writing many now-
famous Buddhist texts including *Bodhicaryavatara* and
The Path of Light.

Options:

- Consider saying this prayer while kneeling, with hands
  folded, adding a prostration at the end of each line.
  This is a deep form of reverence and humility, and is
  part of the Islamic tradition.

- If you are saying this prayer in the early hours, you may wish to carry the italicized line in memory, throughout the rest of the day, repeating it silently as your mantra.

- Repeat the italicized line on your wrist mala throughout the day, reflecting on how each of your actions reflects this resolve.

Tradition/Path: Hinduism

May That One

May that one Para Brahman of the Hindus,

Allah of the Muhammadans,

Buddha of the Buddhists,

Ahur Mazda of the Zoroastrians,

Jehovah of the Jews,

Father in Heaven of the Christians,

The Divine Mother of the Shaktas,

Grant unto us all,

Peace, Wisdom, Prosperity, and Immortality.

Origin:

Sri Swami Sivananda (1887–1963), a yogi-meditation teacher and the founder of the Divine Light Society.

Options:

- Use this devotion at the start of each week, creating the intention to honor the holiness of all spiritual paths.

- Your practice shouldn't require external items. Create an interior altar in your imagination, a prayer place within your spirit that you can withdraw to anytime. Imagine yourself kneeling on your prayer rug, wearing your prayer shawl, taking inspiration from the statues and icons on your altar, inhaling the incense, delighting in the flicker of the candles, placing flowers on the altar that reflect the season, listening to the music you have chosen. Close your eyes and allow your heart to open to God alone.

I Offer

I offer my body, my speech, and my mind

The best I have to give,

Both actually arranged here before you and
   imagined

Multiplied millions of times to fill the space
   between us.

I regret and vow never to repeat actions that
   caused suffering

I rejoice in those that caused happiness.

I request you the enlightened beings

To remain till I become like you.

I request your wise and compassionate guidance

And dedicate any merit to benefit all beings.

Origin:

A traditional Buddhist prayer said before meditation.

Options:

- If you have a chime or singing bowl, sound it at the start of each line.

- Choose one vow, offering, or request from the prayer and make this your focus or intention for the day.

- Non-Buddhists may omit the italicized line or create one reflecting their own tradition.

Tradition/Path: Judaism

Only Thou

Wherever I go—only Thou!

Wherever I stand—only Thou!

Just Thou! Again Thou! Always Thou!

Thou! Thou! Thou!

When things are good—Thou!

When things are bad—Thou!

Thou! Thou! Thou! Thou!

Origin:

An early Hasidic song. Hasidic Judaism is a theologically conservative form of Judaism.

Options:

- Are you immersed in God? All activities are a source of blessing if we are connected with our Source. Choose a routine activity and focus all of your attention, reflecting on how it connects you with all of creation.

- Wear a bracelet or rubber band and snap it saying "Only Thou" whenever you need to remind yourself you are in your Creator and He or She is in you at this very moment.

Tradition/Path: Buddhism

May I Become

May I become at all times, both now and forever,

A protector for those without protection

A guide for those who have lost their way

A ship for those with oceans to cross

A bridge for those with rivers to cross

A sanctuary for those in danger

A lamp for those without light

A place of refuge for those who lack shelter

And a servant to all in need.

Origin:

Traditional Buddhist prayer.

Options:

- If you pray with a partner, take turns reading alternate lines. Choose one line and see how you can actualize this aspect of the vow today. Can you be a lamp for those without light?

- Use "May I Become" as a centering prelude to meditation. Choose a significant word from the prayer, such as "protector" or "sanctuary," to help clear your mind while you meditate.

- Add a salutation and closing to reflect your spiritual path.

Tradition/Path: African

In the Beginning

In the beginning was God,

Today is God,

Tomorrow will be God,

Who can make an image of God?

He has no body.

He is a word which comes out of your mouth.

That word! It is no more,

It is past, and it still lives!

So is God.

Origin:

This creed-type devotion, which echoes the Christian opening of the Gospel of John, is recited by the Pygmies of the African Congo to acknowledge the eternal spirit that is the Creator.

Options:

- Try this creed to replace one you usually say to begin your day or profess during the day. Consider occasionally saying other creeds to keep your mind and heart awake to the process.

- Use the italicized passage as an arrow prayer.

- Create a mandala as you pray, using paper and crayons, sand, or colored beads. You may return to your devotional creation, adding new touches each day. Keep it on your altar.

Thou Art

Thou art my mother and my father thou art,

Thou art my brother and my friend thou art,

Thou art my knowledge, my wealth thou art.

Thou art my everything, my God of Gods.

Origin:

From the original Sanskrit, this is a traditional prayer said at the end of *Satsang* (Sanskrit for "in the company of people"), usually at the end of the day to close the day by clarifying the mind and reconnecting with the source from which our energy originates.

Options:

- Keep a tithing box at your prayer place and give back to God as you read "my wealth thou art." At the end of a specified period, contribute your tithe to a charity close to your heart.

- Use this prayer as a Communion/Holy Eucharist prayer if you are a Christian.

- Try "Thou Art" as a mantra or on prayer beads (repeating the prayer as many times as you have beads).

Tradition/Path: Catholic Christian

Emptied of Myself

Sever me from myself that I may be grateful to you;

May I perish to myself that I may be safe in you;

May I die to myself that I may live in you;

May I wither to myself that I may blossom in you;

May I be emptied of myself that I may abound in you;

May I be nothing to myself that I may be all to you.

Origin:

Erasmus (ca. 1469–1536), Dutch humanist, Latin scholar, and Roman Catholic priest.

Options:

- This prayer lends itself well to prayer beads. Pause to read a scriptural reading from the tradition of your choice at the end of each decade.

- Use any one of the lines to carry with you today as a silent mantra.

- Select a line that speaks to you and use it for a *lectio divina* reflection for your morning or evening prayer.

Tradition/Path: Christian

Apostles' Creed, Updated

I believe in God, Creator, Redeemer, and Sanctifier,

The God who calls us together in a holy Catholic Church—

Welcoming all, including all, embracing all—

A community of faith, hope, and love,

A community of nonviolence,

A community of resisters and peacemakers.

A community of children, women, and men.

Black, brown, red, yellow, and white,

Of every variety and age and land—

To walk together in peace and love.

I believe that we shall join the communion of saints,

From Mary and Joseph, Peter and Paul,

To Francis and Clare,

Ignatius of Loyola and Thérèse of Lisieux,

To Dorothy Day and Mohandas Gandhi,

Martin Luther King, Jr. and Thea Bowman.

Oscar Romero and Ignacio Ellacurta,

Franz Jaegerstaetter and Thomas Merton,

Ita Ford and Maura Clarke,

Dorothy Kazel and Jean Donovan,

And the whole cloud of witnesses—

All martyrs, prophets, apostles, and
   peacemakers—

The whole of humanity in the great dance of life.

I believe in the God of life and the resurrection.

I believe. God.

Help my unbelief.

   Amen. Alleluia.

Origin:

John Dear, SJ, peace activist and author of numerous books on peace and justice, including *Mary of Nazareth, Prophet of Peace* (Ave Maria Press).

Options:

- If you have special saints, holy persons, or ancestors you wish to remember, add them to the list of names or replace those names with yours.

- Say this prayer on mala beads, one line to a bead.

- Sound a singing bowl as you read the name of each holy person. Pause after each name to let the ringing tone of the bowl die away.

Praise and Devotion

Tradition/Path: Buddhism

Offerings to the Buddha

Reverencing the Buddha, we offer flowers,

Flowers that today are fresh and sweetly blooming,

Flowers that tomorrow are faded and fallen.

Our bodies, too, like flowers, will pass away.

Reverencing the Buddha, we offer candles.

To Him who is the Light, we offer light.

From his greater lamp a lesser lamp we light within
us,

The lamp of wisdom shining within our hearts.

Reverencing the Buddha, we offer incense,

Incense whose fragrance pervades the air,

The fragrance of the perfect life, sweeter than
incense,

Spreads in all directions throughout the world.

Origin:

Theravada Buddhist scriptures (sixth to third century
B.C.), which are thought to contain the earliest
surviving record of the Buddha's teaching.

Options:

- Light incense or a candle before saying this prayer. Consider keeping a few fresh flowers or even a few herbal plants at your altar or prayer mat.

- Substitute the name of your higher power for "Buddha."

- If you pray three times daily, use one verse for each prayer time.

Buddha

Divine Seamstress

Divine seamstress.
We are the garment
You have stitched with love
To clothe your holy child.
We are the swaddling cloth
And the robe of one piece
Torn by the failure of human compassion.
Enable us by your presence within us
To show forth the hope of Christ;
That suffering and oppression end,
And the hearts of people everywhere
Beat with the fullness of your joy.
To you be praise,
Great Mother,
Vulnerable Child,
Spirit of Love,
One Divinity now and forever.
Amen.

Origin:

Mary Kathleen Speegle Schmitt, a contemporary Anglican priest and author of *Seasons of the Feminine Divine*. She was inspired by Proverbs 31:10–31 (NJB) which speaks of "The truly capable woman . . . who holds out her hands to the poor, who opens her arms to the needy."

Options:

- "You need not cry very loud, He is very near," said Post-Reformation mystic Brother Lawrence. So is she, and we need to know the feminine nurturing aspects of God to know God fully. See God as the Great Mother today.

- Use the italicized passages for one or more of your prayer breaks today to deepen your sensitivity to the suffering in the world.

Tradition/Path: Catholic Christian

Jesus in Silence

Let us adore Jesus in our hearts,

Who spent thirty years out of thirty-three in silence;

Who began his public life by spending forty days in silence;

Who often retired alone to spend the night on a mountain in silence.

He who spoke with authority,

Now spends his earthly life in silence.

Let us adore Jesus in the Eucharistic silence.

Origin:

Mother Teresa of Calcutta, founder of the Sisters of Charity (1910–1997); she was beatified in 2004.

Options:

- Use this as a prayer before meditation. Use the figure of Jesus meditating in silence as your focus.

- Spend a small block of time each day over the next forty days in silence, dedicated to Jesus. Record your observations in your journal about how the habit of holy silence has affected or changed you.

Tradition/Path: Catholic Christian

Your Holy Name

What can I say to you, My God? Shall I collect together all the words that praise your holy Name?

Shall I give you all the names of this world, you, the Unnameable?

Shall I call you, God of my life, meaning of my existence, hallowing of my acts,

My journey's end, bitterness of my bitter hours,

Home of my loneliness, you my most treasured happiness?

Shall I say:

You the All-merciful, you the Just One, you Love itself? *Creator, Sustainer, Pardoner, Near One, Distant One,*

Incomprehensible One, God both of flowers and stars,

God of the gentle wind and of terrible battles, Wisdom, Power, Loyalty and Truthfulness,

Eternity and Infinity.

Origin:

Karl Rahner, SJ (1904–1984). A Jesuit priest, Rahner was one of the most influential theologians of the Vatican II era, and is the author of many works including *Foundations of Christian Faith* and *Prayers for a Lifetime.*

Options:

- Experiment with a different way of praying: if you pray silently, say this prayer aloud, hearing the music of Rahner's poetic prose.

- Consider the many names of God, beginning with those italicized in this prayer. Which names do you use for God? Develop a more expansive relationship with God by using a new name each day expressing his/her infinite aspects.

Tradition/Path: Christian

Beyond

Eternal, incomprehensible God,

I believe, and confess, and adore Thee,

As being infinitely more wonderful,

Resourceful and immense,

Than this universe I see.

Origin:

John Henry Newman (1801–1890), Cardinal-Deacon of the Basilica of Saint George in Velabro, in Rome. He began his vocation as an Anglican and ended it as a Roman Catholic cardinal. He was a philosopher, scholar, and leader of the Oxford Movement (a High Church effort to return to the foundations of the faith) of the late 1800s.

Options:

- Consider adding sound to your prayer time. Add a small bell or chime to your prayer mat or altar. Ring it gently to signal the start of your devotions, marking the transition from the external world to your internal essential self. Ring it again, marking your movement from the interior sacred space to the world.

- Carry a copy of this prayer with you or keep a copy in your car to bring your attention back to God from time to time during the day.

Centering Prayer

There are times when I am with you

When there is no beginning or ending of time:

When the day is dateless

And the rhythm of time

Has ceased to record the hours

And the calendar, the days;

When no birds sing, but rest;

And no winds blow, but breathe.

And the air is drenched

With the white silence of love

And my fingers trace

The lineaments of Your Face.

Origin:

Brother Thomas Moore Page, CFX (Congregation of Xaverian Brothers).

Options:

- Use this as a centering prayer before meditation. Can you leave ordinary time behind and sink into God's time?

- Use the italicized passage as a reflection throughout the day. Take the feeling of the spaciousness of sacred time with you today.

Tradition/Path: Christian Feminism

Wheel of Life

Ancient woman,

You spin out creation

On the Wheel of Life,

And our beginning and end

Feel the rough skin of your hands.

When the sun fails,

And the moon goes dark,

Gather your children

From the ends of the earth;

That, redeemed by your compassion,

All humanity may enter the home

That You have prepared for us;

Lady of the Four Winds,

Uniter of Heaven and Earth,

One Who Brings Us Home,

Amen.

Origin:

Mary Kathleen Speegle Schmitt, a contemporary Anglican priest and author of *Seasons of the Feminine Divine.*

Options:

- We limit our experience of our genderless God when we limit the names and descriptives we use for the Creator. Become comfortable with the new names italicized and create some of your own. Substitute them in the prayers you regularly pray. Note how this changes your experience of speaking with and to God.

- Experiment by changing your mental image of God— try seeing the Creator as African, Asian, Native American, a young woman, or an older woman. How does this change your attitude in prayer?

Thou are my Lord;
I have no good
beyond Thee.

Psalm 16:2 (RV)

Affirmations and Intentions

Tradition/Path: Buddhism

Boundless Love

Let no one deceive another.

Let no one anywhere despise another.

Let no one out of anger or resentment

Wish suffering on anyone at all.

Just as a mother with her own life

Protects her child, her only child, from harm,

So within yourself let grow

A boundless love for all creatures.

Origin:

Sutta-nipata, or "The Discourse Collection," is a text containing some of the oldest and most profound discourses of the Buddha. It is the fifth book (out of fifteen total) of the *Khuddaka Nikaya,* or "Collection of Little Texts."

Options:

- Reflect on the concept of boundless love and how you can "within yourself let [it] grow" this day, and keep it growing around you.

- Close with a Native American Amen, I Ask This for Myself, My People, and All My Relations, or the Buddhist Om.

This Fleeting World

The Radiant Buddha said:

Regard this fleeting world like this:

Like stars fading and vanishing at dawn,

Like bubbles on a fast moving stream,

Like morning dewdrops evaporating on blades
   of grass,

Like a candle, flickering in a strong wind,

Echoes, mirages, and phantoms, hallucinations,

And like a dream.

Origin:

Called *The Eight Similes of Illusion*, this teaching from the Prajna Paramita Sutras, a collection of Buddhist precepts, is often chanted by meditators. It reflects the attitude of the Buddha who often referred to earthly existence as "This *saha* [insubstantial, incomprehensible] world."

Options:

- This is an excellent devotion to read while doing a mindfulness walk outdoors in the morning or early evening.

- Christians may change the first line to read "O Lord, I regard," then add at the end, "We look for You and life everlasting, Amen."

Tradition/Path: Native American

Hold On

I will hold on to what is good

And I will hold on to what I believe

Even when it is a tree which stands by itself.

And I will hold on to what I must do,

Even if it is a long way from here.

I will hold on to life, even when it is easier to let go.

Please hold on to my hand, even when I have gone
away from you.

Origin:

Adapted from a prayer by an unknown Pueblo Indian
supplicant.

Options:

- Say "Hold On" as a morning prayer for courage for the
day.

- Keep a copy of this prayer taped to your computer or
in your car for strength in "difficult" moments.

- You may add a salutation of your choice and an Amen
or alternative to close the prayer.

- Read this prayer aloud facing yourself in a mirror to
deepen the meaning of the words you are reading.

Like a Wind

Great Spirit, Creator Mother of the World,

    Like a wind you seem to be always drawing near
      and passing by

    To empower your creatures toward life and
      well-being

    In the teeth of the antagonistic structures in
      our political reality.

Welcome, Spirit of Hope!

Welcome, Sophia-Wisdom!

Welcome, Empowering Strength,

    She who is and will always be,

Free, loving, and infinitely creative.

Origin:

Elizabeth A. Johnson, CSJ, Christian feminist author
and professor of Theology at Fordham University, in
New York City.

Sophia is Greek for "wisdom." Sophia is also the name
given by Paul to Jesus in First Corinthians 1:24 where
he refers to Jesus as "the Sophia of God." Presented as
a powerful, wise, just, and saving woman in the Biblical
book of Sirach, Sophia combines the practical wisdom
of women—referred to as *Hokmah* in Hebrew—with
the ability to guide and counsel with universal wisdom
and knowledge.

Options:

- Take a few minutes to center yourself. If you keep a bowl of blessing water on your altar or prayer place, use this now.

- You may wish to invoke the names of holy women who have inspired you after the italicized passage. Keep their names or images on your prayer altar.

- Think about God in a new way today as "Creator Mother of the World."

Womb of Mystery

I pray to you,

. . . the womb of mystery

The birther of new life

The breast of unending delight

The passionate embrace of woman

The emanation of feminine beauty

The Mother of Creation

The cosmic dance of Sophia Wisdom

The sister of courage, justice, and peace

The feminine face of God

I have longed to kiss.

Origin:

Adapted from the poem by Bridget Meehan, SSC. The Society of Sisters for the Church (SSC) is a new Catholic ecclesial community for women who have left more traditional orders but want to stay in religious life and serve new needs.

Options:

- Christian Feminist theologian Elizabeth Johnson believes that "The very incomprehensibility of God demands a proliferation of images and a variety of names . . . [to] act as a corrective against the tendency of any one to become reified and literal." Reflect on your image of God as you read this prayer, then create a feminine image of God for your altar or prayer corner.

- Gather a list of names of your "sister[s] of courage, justice, and peace," women who have done great things in the name of the Holy One. Post that list on or near your prayer place as a reminder of the strong women in your life.

Tradition/Path: Transdenominational

Seeking Truth

I am a seeker of truth on a spiritual journey.

I believe life has sacred meaning and purpose.

May my behavior today express my deepest beliefs,

May I approach each and every task today with quiet impeccability.

May I be a simple, humble, kind presence on the earth today.

May I see the Divine Nature in all beings today.

May I be grateful today to those who came before me,

And may I make the roads smoother for those who will travel them after me.

May I leave each place at least a little better than I found it today.

May I truly cherish this day, knowing that it may be my last.

May I remember, remember, remember, not to forget, forget, forget.

Origin:

Bo Lozoff, cofounder and director of the Human Kindness Foundation and the award-winning Prison-Ashram Project. The Human Kindness Foundation (www.humankindness.org) is a nonprofit organization that promotes a way of life based on three common principles taught by the great sages of all religions: simple living, a dedication to service, and a commitment to personal spiritual practice.

Options:

- Read this prayer in the morning for clarification of your motivations as you move through your day. Speak each line slowly, reflecting on its meaning.

- God is closer than your breath. Breathe mindfully, using conscious slow rhythmic inhalations and exhalations, as you read each line.

- Choose one of the intentions in this prayer to carry with you for the next twenty-four hours. Write it down and resolve to perform all your actions today with this intention.

- Light one tea light or votive candle for each intention above as you read it, pausing after the last line to note a thing, person, or occasion you wish "not to forget" today.

Tradition/Path: Buddhismz

Hearts in Friendship

May the poor find wealth,

Those weak with sorrow find joy,

May the forlorn find new hope,

Constant happiness, and prosperity.

May the frightened cease to be afraid,

And those bound be free.

May the weak find power,

And may their hearts join in friendship.

Origin:

His Holiness the fourteenth (and present) Dalai Lama.
His name means "Ocean of Wisdom" in Tibetan.

Options:

- In the Buddhist practice *tonglen* ("sending and taking"),
  one imagines giving the source of all joy to another
  person or creature, thereby removing their suffering. It
  is believed that through a genuine sense of caring and
  compassion, our sharing in their plight, we can indeed
  help reduce that suffering. Practice tonglen while you
  say the words of this affirmation. With practice you
  will notice an increase in your own strength and
  courage.

- Try this prayer as a breathing practice, breathing in on
  the first line, breathing out on the next.

- Hold in your mind and heart some particular person
  or group of beings who are suffering as you slowly say
  this prayer.

Tradition/Path: East Asian/Nondenominational

All Things Are My Companions

Heaven is my father and earth my mother

And even such a small creature as I,

Finds an intimate place in its midst.

That which extends throughout the universe, I regard
as my body

And that which directs the universe, I regard as my
nature.

All people are my brothers and sisters

And all things are my companions.

Mani prayer stone

Origin:

An inscription on the wall
of the workplace of an
eleventh-century Chinese
administrative official.

Options:

- This prayer may be recited on a mala
  or rosary, one line to a bead, and repeated until all the
  beads have been said.

- The italicized passages above may be used
  independently as a meditation focus or as mantras.

- Try opening and closing this prayer with the Buddhist
  Om Mani Padme Hum. Think about each of the six
  perfections (p. 24) as you say this prayer.

But One

I am but one,

But I am one.

I cannot do everything,

But I can do something.

What I can do,

I ought to do.

What I ought to do,

By the grace of God,

I will do.

Lord, what wilt thou have me do?

Origin:

This prayer is said daily by the Daughters of the King, a woman's service group within the Episcopal Church of the United States.

Options:

- Use this prayer as an impetus to get involved. Try helping out at a local charity a few hours a week.

- To use "But One" as a secular affirmation, omit the italicized lines or make your own substitutions.

- Following Islamic and Orthodox Jewish custom, pause several times daily to pray this prayer, or selected lines that you have memorized.

Tradition/Path: Earth Spirituality

World Below

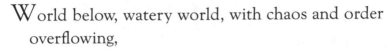

World below, watery world, with chaos and order overflowing,

Bring true creation into my life, with order and beauty,

With power and grace.

World above, far-flung heavens, ordering the world

With might and law,

Bring true stability into my life, with law and structure,

With clarity and reason.

World about me, far-extending, with land well-set,

Bring true being into my life, with help and love,

With health and prosperity.

Origin:

Unknown

Options:

- Find a holy place outside or a place you have made holy by praying there and speak the words of this prayer after quieting yourself. Listen to the messages of creation. Listen with your whole body and soul. Does a wind blowing over a stone sound like something speaking to you? Does the sun striking a tree raise a scent from the bark? What about the light on moving water?

- Sit beside a creek, pond, or even a bowl of water on a clear evening. Follow the motions of the prayer in the reflection of the water as you read and enact it.

Tradition/Path: Christian

Our Life Is Seed

Our life is seed,

Sown in the earth to rise again

In the world to come,

Where we will be renewed by Christ

In immortal life.

I did not frame this body,

Nor will I destroy it;

God, you gave me life,

You will also restore it.

Origin:

Saint Jonas of Hubaham, Persian monk and early martyr of the Christian church. His Feast Day is March 29.

Options:

- Grow something from seed and keep it at your prayer place. An easy annual to start from seed is the zinnia. Let your plant's growth pace the growth in your prayer life.

- Use this prayer as a mealtime grace, thanking God for the life-restoring food you are about to eat.

- Alter the prayer and add an opening salutation and a closing to reflect your beliefs.

Tradition/Path: Christian

Jesus Taught Me

The world told me that I was only a spark,

But Jesus taught me that I am a fire.

The world told me that I was only a string,

But Jesus taught me that I am a lyre.

The world told me that I was only an anthill,

But Jesus taught me that I am a mountain.

The world told me that I was only a drop,

But Jesus told me that I am a fountain.

The world told me that I was only a feather,

But Jesus taught me that I am a wing.

The world told me that I was only a beggar,

But Jesus taught me that I am a king.

Origin:

Anonymous

Options:

- If you are not a Christian, you may substitute the name of your higher power for "Jesus."

- Use any two lines beginning with "The world told me" as a journaling exercise. Take a few minutes to ponder the meaning of each line, then record your thoughts (considered or freeform) in your journal.

● Bring the Holy Trinity into this devotion by making the sign of the cross before each new thought in the prayer. The cross may have a different symbolism for you if you are not Christian. Invoke this meaning as you bless yourself.

cross

Tradition/Path: Christian Feminism

O Holy Memory

O Holy Memory,

Carry us down the ages

On threads of remembrance,

Connect us with our sisters

And mothers of all times.

Bring us their childhood innocence

And their adolescent hope again.

Recreate the longings of our mothers and
   grandmothers

Before their succumbing

To the weight of patriarchy.

Touch us with the unfulfilled

Capacities of our foremothers

Whose lost energies we now resurrect.

Gather the light threads

Of anguish and hope

That bind us together

And weave for us a new memory

In this time and place.

Blessed Be.

230

Origin:

Evelyn Hunt, from *WomenPsalms*, compiled by Julia Ahlers, Rosemary Broughton, and Carl Koch.

Options:

- Bring this prayer alive by awakening your holy memory of women (mothers, sisters, grandmothers, mentors) who have been important, transformative in your life. Hold them in your heart as you say this prayer, speaking their names aloud at the appropriate moments.

- To connect you with your "sisters and mothers of all times," keep an icon, drawing, photo, statue, or reminder of a holy heroine (from real life or history) at your prayer corner and change it from time to time.

Grant us grace,
Almighty Father,

So to pray as to deserve
to be heard.

Jane Austen

Tradition/Path: Hinduism

Perfect Be Our Unity

O God, let us be united;

Let us speak in harmony;

Let our minds apprehend alike;

Common be our prayer,

Common the end of our assembly;

Common be our resolution;

Common be our deliberation.

Alike be our feelings;

Unified be our hearts;

Common be our intentions;

Perfect be our unity.

Origin:

From the Rig Veda, one of four Vedas. The Vedas are the primary texts of Hinduism. They contain hymns, incantations, and rituals.

Options:

- Form the intention to act always with *agape* (unconditional love) toward all beings as you say this prayer.

- Close the prayer with Svaha, Namaste, or Om Shanti, Shanti, Shanti.

- After reading this prayer, take a moment to record your spontaneous thoughts in your prayer journal.

Tradition/Path: Catholic Christian

Only Today

My life is an instant,

An hour which passes by;

My life is a moment

Which I have no power to stay.

You know, O, my God,

That to love you here on earth—

I have only today.

Origin:

Saint Thérèse of Lisieux (1873–1897) is often called the "little flower." She defined her path to God and holiness as "The Little Way," which consisted of love and trust in God.

Options:

- If you pray the Hours, use this prayer each time you pause to bring you into the present where God is always present.

- If you have a mindfulness-based practice like yoga or Tai Chi, say this prayer before you begin.

Tradition/Path: Christian

For Virtues

Make me, Lord

Obedient without complaint

Poor without regret

Patient without murmur

Humble without pretense

Joyful without foolishness

Truthful without disguise.

Origin:

Saint Thomas Aquinas (1225–1274), one of the great theologians of the Christian church, whose best known work, a systematic summary combining secular philosophy and theology, is the *Summa Theologica*.

Options:

- Use "For Virtues" as a morning prayer. Select one line as your intention for the day.

- Read this prayer aloud, a practice that turns prayer into a tangible conversation with God.

Litanies and Mantras

Tradition/Path: Islam

Your Holy Names

Most gracious Lord, Master, Messiah, and Savior
of humanity,

We greet You with all humility.

You are the First Cause and the First Effect,

The Divine Light and the Spirit of Guidance,

Alpha and Omega.

Your Light is in all forms, Your love in all beings:

In a loving mother, in a kind father,

In an innocent child,

In a helpful friend,

In an inspiring teacher.

Allow us to recognize You in all Your holy names
and forms:

As Rama, as Krishna, as Shiva, as Buddha.

Let us know You as Abraham, as Solomon, as
Zarathustra,

As Moses, as Jesus, as Muhammad,

And in many other names and forms,

Known and unknown in the world.

We adore Your past;

Your Presence deeply enlightens our being, and we
look for Your blessing in the future,

O Messenger, Christ, Nabi, the Rasul of God!

You Whose heart constantly reaches upward,

You come on earth with a Message,

As a dove from above when Dharma decays,

And speaks the Word that is put into Your
mouth,

As the light fills the crescent moon.

Let the star of the Divine Light shining in Your
heart

Be reflected in the hearts of Your devotees.

May the Message of God reach far and wide, ·

Illuminating and making the whole humanity

As one single brotherhood in the Fatherhood of
God.

Amen.

Origin:

Adapted from *Salat,* by Hazrat Pir-o-Murshid Inayat
Khan (1882–1927), founder of the Sufi Order in the
West. His teaching emphasized the fundamental
oneness of all religions. ("Hazrat" is an honorific; "Pir-
o-Murshid" is an esoteric title signifying his position.)

Options:

- Use the World Peace Prayer Society's arrow prayer,
  "May Peace Prevail on Earth," as a closing for this
  prayer.

- Expand your spirituality. Learn something about one
  of the spiritual teachers and prophets unfamiliar to
  you in this prayer.

Tradition/Path: Earth Spirituality

Soul of Our Souls (Four Prayers)

I.

Divine Air—bring imagination and creativity to the world.

Like the far-seeing hawk,

May we see this situation as the whole complex tapestry that it is,

And be inspired with fresh and virgin weavings.

Like the unfettered winds,

May we be freed from old assumptions and patterns in how we respond,

And breathe in new possibilities.

II.

Divine Fire—bring clarity and compassionate passion to the world.

Like the bright light of the sun,

May we see clearly the way forward of "what is necessary" for all life,

And the time to come.

Like the transforming flames,

May our grief, fear, and rage be transformed into compassion for all—

All victims and perpetrators alike.

III.

Divine Water—bring yielding and wisdom to the world.

Like the gentle erosion of water upon stone,

May we release our personal and cultural biases,

And acknowledge the "wrong-thinkings" that we may harbor.

Like the deepening twilight upon the earth,

May we remember the lessons of the past,

And contemplate their meanings for the future.

IV.

Divine Earth—bring greening and surety to the world.

Like the stretching branches of the tree,

May we stretch ourselves

Into the life-affirming paths of reconciliation and healing.

Like the deep peaceful dome of night,

May we stand firm in the Goddess and the God,

Through this "dark night" of confusion and fear, and false "stars."

May our souls be strong, steady, and revealing.

May our spirits be enlightened, faithful, and sure.

May our choices be wise and enduring, for the generations to come.

By all that is Sacred and True,

So Mote it Be.

Origin:

Pashta MaryMoon, cofounder of the Pagan Pastoral Outreach Association, which provides pastoral services to prisons and hospitals on behalf of the Pagan community.

This prayer was taken from The World Prayers Project (www.worldprayers.org), a not-for-profit Web site that collects unique and rare prayers from around the world for the purpose of inspiration, study, and cross -cultural appreciation.

Options:

- Combine your reading with a walking meditation in nature.

- Use the italicized passage as an arrow prayer to say at any time during the day.

- There are many possibilities here for even a secular *lectio divina.* Choose one sentence or passage that speaks to you and sit with it, journaling if you like.

Tradition/Path: Catholic Christian

Litany of Mary of Nazareth

Glory to you, God our Creator . . .
    Breathe into us new life, new meaning.

Glory to you, God our Savior . . .
    Lead us in the way of peace and justice.

Glory to you, healing Spirit . . .
    Transform us to empower others.

Mary wellspring of peace . . . Be our guide.

Model of strength,

Model of gentleness,

Model of trust,

Model of courage,

Model of patience,

Model of risk,

Model of openness,

Model of perseverance,

Mother of the liberator . . . Pray for us.

Mother of the homeless,

Mother of the dying,

Mother of the nonviolent,

Widowed mother,

Unwed mother,

Mother of a political prisoner,

Mother of the condemned,

Mother of an executed criminal,

Oppressed woman . . . Lead us to life.

Liberator of the oppressed,

Marginalized woman,

Comforter of the afflicted,

Cause of our joy,

Sign of contradiction,

Breaker of bondage,

Political refugee,

Seeker of sanctuary,

First Disciple,

Sharer in Christ's passion,

Seeker of God's will,

Witness to Christ's resurrection,

Woman of mercy . . . Empower us.

Woman of faith,

Woman of contemplation,
   Woman of vision,

Woman of wisdom and understanding,

Woman of grace and truth,

Woman, pregnant with hope,

Woman, centered in God,

Mary, Queen of Peace,

We entrust our lives to you.

Shelter us from war, hatred, and oppression.

Teach us to live in peace,

To educate ourselves for peace.

Inspire us to act justly,

To revere all God has made.

Root peace firmly in our hearts and in our world.

Origin:

Pax Christi USA, a national Catholic peace movement that promotes nonviolence and social justice.

Options:

- Recite this prayer using a mala or prayer rope.

- If you pray regularly to Mary you may wish to add the Catholic Hail Mary and the Magnificat (Luke 1:46–55) to your prayer time.

- Use an icon, statue, or other likeness of the Mother of God to reflect upon while you recite this prayer.

He hath shown his mercy unto me.

In peace I walk the straight road.

Cheynne (Lotus 118)

Tradition/Path: Catholic Christian

Come Spirit of God

Come Spirit of God,* grant us

The power to be gentle,

The strength to be forgiving,

The patience to be understanding,

The endurance to accept the consequences

Of holding on to what is right.

Come Spirit of God,* help us to put our trust in

The power of good to overcome evil,

The power of love to overcome hatred.

Come Spirit of God,* enlighten us

With the vision to see and the faith to believe in

A world free from violence,

A new world where fear will no longer lead us

To commit injustices,

Nor selfishness cause us to bring suffering to
others.

Come Spirit of wisdom and love,*

Source of all good, teach us your truth

And guide our actions in your way of peace.

Amen.

Origin:

Adapted from "A Prayer to the Holy Spirit" from *Prayers for Peacemakers*, for Pax Christi USA. Pax Christi USA is a national Catholic peace movement that promotes nonviolence and social justice.

Options:

- Set a small bowl of blessing water near your prayer area. Dip your fingers into the bowl at the beginning of each stanza to bless yourself, commissioning yourself into the reign of God's justice.

- Use each of the four stanzas as a separate prayer. Think how you might actualize this reflection today, this week.

- Read the prayer aloud, sounding your singing bowl at each marked star (*). Let the tone reverberate and slowly die away as you silently call for the Creator to bless your prayer time.

singing bowl and mallet

Tradition/Path: Buddhism

Loving Kindness

· ·

May I be filled with loving kindness,

May I be well.

May I be peaceful and at ease.

May I be happy.

Origin:

Loving-kindness is a 2,500-year-old meditation practice taught by the Buddha to develop the mental habit of selfless or altruistic love.

Options:

- Begin by repeating the words over and over for ten minutes once or twice a day. Focus on yourself for the first week. Let whatever feelings arise permeate your body and mind. After a week begin to include loved ones in your meditation. After another week include friends, community members, and neighbors. Eventually embrace all beings everywhere.

- Use this meditation silently while stuck in traffic or while waiting in a long line—difficult situations where your patience is tried.

- Place both hands over your heart as you pray. Focus on opening your heart as you open your hands out to the world, sending your heart's energy.

Tradition/Path: Hinduism

Om Shanti

···

May the Lord of Love protect us

May the Lord of Love nourish us

May the Lord of Love strengthen us

May we realize the Lord of Love.

May we live with love for all;

May we live in peace for all.

Om Shanti, Shanti, Shanti.

Origin:

The Upanishads, the teachings of the sages on mystical experience. They are part of the Vedas (sacred Hindu scripture).

Options:

- "Om Shanti" may be said on prayer beads. For example, if you are using the decades of a rosary, say the prayer five times.

- Light a small votive candle as you recite each line, pausing to reflect. If you are praying in a group, each line can be said by a different person, who then lights a candle.

- Add your own intercessions starting with, "May I . . . (find rest in your love, etc.)."

Resources

Religious Traditions

The Web sites listed below have been provided to help you learn more about the Paths cited in this book.

Anglican/Episcopal Christian
www.anglicancommunion.org
www.ecusa.anglican.org

Buddhism
www.buddhanet.net

Catholicism
www.americancatholic.org

Christian Feminism
david.snu.edu/~dwilliam.fs/f97projects/xnfem/html/ frames2.html

Christian Science
www.tfccs.com

Christianity
geneva.rutgers.edu/src/christianity/

Earth Spirituality
www.amystickalgrove.com

Eastern Orthodox
www.oca.org

Hinduism
www.himalayanacademy.com

Islam
www.theislamproject.com

Judaism
www.jewfaq.org

Native American
www.native-languages.org/religion.htm

Shinto
www.religioustolerance.org/shinto.htm

Sufism
www.ias.org/

Taoism
www.truetao.org

Theosophy
www.theosophical.org

Zoroastrianism
www.zoroastrianism.com

Prayerware

The Web sites listed below have been provided to help you find the items of prayerware mentioned and used in this book.

Dharmashop.com

http://dharmashop.com

Prayer rugs, mala, wrist malas, singing bowls, incense, etc.

Dharmashop.com supports Tibetan artisans by buying directly from Tibetan communities in Nepal and India. A portion of all proceeds is donated to charity.

Gaiam, Inc.
www.gaiam.com

Yoga and fitness tools, meditation supplies, whole foods, etc.

Gaiam was created to offer options for people who want to live a more natural and healthy life with respect for the environment.

Hither and Yon
www.hitherandyononline.com

Mani stones, mantra carvings, Tibetan incense, etc.

Hither and Yon purchases their items directly from artisans in Asia.

Israelcraft, The Tallit Shop
www.israelcraft.com/

Handpainted silk Jewish prayer shawls

The Web site includes information about how to wear the shawl, the history behind the shawl, and the rituals for using it in prayer.

Just Rosaries
http://justrosaries.gray-cells.com

Rosaries, rosary bracelets, etc.

Just Rosaries makes and donates a Ranger Rosary to the men and women of the United States Military with every order placed. For each order of $25.00 or more they also make and donate a Mission Rosary to a family rosary program called Rosaries for the World.

Karma Khameleon
www.kharmakhameleon.com

Tingshas, singing bowls, drums, altar cards and statues, etc.

Many of the items sold here protect the culture and support the peoples of Tibet living in Nepal and India in refugee camps.

Labyrinthos
www.labyrinthos.net

Books, information about locating labyrinths, etc.

Labyrinthos details the history of the labyrinth, contains images of modern labyrinths, and offers consultation services for designing your own labyrinth.

The Monastery Store
www.dharma.net/monstore/

Prayer cushions, altar supplies, statues, incense supplies, instruments, etc.

The Monastery Store is the online catalog of Dharma Communications, the not-for-profit educational arm of Zen Mountain Monastery (Buddhism) and the Mountains and Rivers Order located in the Catskill Mountains of New York.

Samadhi Cushions and Store
www.samadhicushions.com

Meditation cushions and benches, gongs, incense, etc.

Samadhi Cushions and Store was founded in 1975 by students of the late Chogyam Trungpa Rinpoche, founder of Shambhala International.

Shambala Mountain
www.shambhalamountain.org/giftstore/index.php

Books, shrine and meditation supplies

Shambhala Mountain is a mountain valley retreat center in Red Feather Lakes, Colorado.

Shawl Ministry
www.shawlministry.com

Prayer shawls

The site includes instructions for creating prayer shawls, instilling them with prayer and good wishes, and giving them as gifts to those in need, whether it be through illness or a special occasion.

Zanzibar Trading Company
www.zanzibar-trading.com

Prayer wheels, singing bowls, tingshas, gongs, etc.

Zanzibar Trading Company imports items directly from more than sixty countries, including Africa, Central America, Tibet, and Nepal.

Acknowledgments

The author has made every attempt to contact all living authors for permission to use the material herewith. Authors who contact the publisher will be properly credited in the next edition.

"All a Circle" by Lynn Andrews. Reprinted with the author's permission.

"An Alternative Lord's Prayer" and "Forgive Us Our Debts" by Neil Douglas-Klotz, from Harper Collins.

"Apostles' Creed, Updated" by John Dear, SJ, from *The Sound of Listening* (Continuum, 1999). Reprinted with the author's permission.

"Break Open Our Hearts" and "She Who Is" by Mary Lou Kownacki, OSB. Reprinted with the permission of the author and Pax Christi USA.

"Come Spirit of God" adapted from "A Prayer to the Holy Spirit" from *Prayers for Peacemakers*, by Pax Christi USA. Used with permission.

"Divine Seamstress," "Heart of Compassion," "One Whose Love Is Enough," "Wheel of Life," "Womb of All," and "Womb of All Creation" by Mary Kathleen Speegle Schmitt. Used with permission.

"For All Things," by Dr. Gail A. Ricciuti. Reprinted with the author's permission.

"God of the Past, Present, and Future" by Rev. Dr. Ralph E. Ahlberg. Reprinted with the author's permission.

"God Who Dances" by Janet Morley, taken from *Bread of Tomorrow*, © Society for Promoting Christian Knowledge. Used with permission.

"Invocation" by John Daido Loori, Zen Mountain Monastery. © Dharma Communications. Used with permission.

FRANCES SHERIDAN GOULART is a part-time yoga coach and Pilates instructor. She has written more than 15 books related to diet and lifestyle. *God Has No Religion* is her first spiritual/devotional book. In addition to the bimonthly column she writes for *Kerux*, the newsletter of Pax Christi Metro New York, her articles have appeared in such publications as *Fellowship in Prayer*, *Focus on the Family*, *Christian Single*, and *Breakaway*. Frances graduated from Hunter College in New York City and now lives in Connecticut.